Published by Applied Research and Design Publishing,
an imprint of ORO Editions.

Gordon Goff: Publisher

www.appliedresearchanddesign.com
info@appliedresearchanddesign.com

Author:
Book Design:
Project Manager: Jake Anderson
10 9 8 7 6 5 4 3 2 1 First Edition
ISBN: 978-1-961856-58-5

Prepress and Print work by ORO Editions Inc.
Printed in China

AR+D Publishing makes a continuous effort to minimize the overall carbon footprint of its publications. As part of this goal, AR+D, in association with Global ReLeaf, arranges to plant trees to replace those used in the manufacturing of the paper produced for its books. Global ReLeaf is an international campaign run by American Forests, one of the world's oldest nonprofit conservation organizations. Global ReLeaf is American Forests' education and action program that helps individuals, organizations, agencies, and corporations improve the local and global environment by planting and caring for trees.

REPRESENTING THE LANDSCAPE PROJECT

THE CREATIVE PROCESS AND DESIGN EDUCATION

DANIELE STEFÀNO

APPLIED RESEARCH +DESIGN

Representing the Landscape Project

The Creative Process and Design Education

Daniele Stefàno

TABLE OF CONTENTS

DESCRIBING AND IMAGINING LANDSCAPES

FOREWORD BY FABIO DI CARLO

This book catches some fundamental issues of landscape architecture, design, and teaching. The thin line that divides the knowledge of real landscapes, the imagination and creation of new ones and their representation, is composed in a process of mirroring between the physical elements and their perception and between concrete figures and desires where all these are linked almost by a bond of consubstantiality: Landscapes and their descriptions are often made of the same material.

In this sense, this work's contents are part of an essential debate, current although not new, with roots both in the more recent past and in the deeper history of a discipline that was originally born within the figurative arts. For over three decades, we have experienced an almost complete conversion that has seen all the branches of the design activities involved in an immersive process inside the digital world. This is a process dominated by a mechanistic presumption of scientific and technical supremacy of digital data. A sort of *neue sachlichkeit*, a new objectivity, which today finds in BIM the expression of a total power of process control where the tool replaces the creative process.

Likewise, in the landscape project, the description increasingly pursues the myth of realism and photorealism through increasingly extreme tools - not yet thoroughly tested - between augmented reality and more, and which perhaps one day will be able to make us feel the smell of the flowers we would like to plant. After 30 years, it is possible to conclude, even from a critical and laic position, which this volume tries to give shape.

First, there is a need for a clear ontological distinction between the purpose of design activities and the purpose of representation, between the role of the contents and that of the different drawing tools. Then, these kits need to be updated to meet the current demands of the landscape project. Among these are ecology and awareness of environmental transition as a constant of an era, according to a consciousness that is no longer anthropocentric but necessarily holistic and inclusive. Here, the project of new ecologies requires other modalities and more open forms of projects that are less crystallized in conception, as in description and communication.

Moreover, understanding that in addition to the virtuosity of hyper-representation, in the relationship with the project users, the need for much more accessible storytelling tools strongly emerges. In this sense, D. Stefàno's work recovers, for example, the role of illustration as a passage and tool that is at the same time friendly but also capable of stimulating suggestion and imagination in different users.

Finally, there is the relationship between landscape imagination and other sciences and disciplines. Leonardo da Vinci already felt the need to represent landscapes with a background but with an autonomous story and dynamic and transformative characteristics. Likewise, Calvino's Invisible Cities, from his novel of the same name, contain richer and more complex landscapes than those of actual cities that can be represented. Nowadays, cognitive sciences and the theory of mirror neurons explain well the role of intangible components in the individual and collective representation of reality.

Therefore, the representation of landscapes today, through the use of a mix of techniques, from the most traditional to the most innovative ones (up to AI), with the most diverse purposes and values, including ethical ones, can return to being an exercise that favors complexity, and return to being a rich experience in the conception, competence, and communication of identity and meanings.

To study an art means to establish its limits, while comparing it with others means emphasizing the same inner tension.

Wassily Kandinsky, *The Spiritual in Art,* 1910.

INTRODUCTION

As we reflect on the role of representation in contemporary landscape design, some questions arise: Why do processes involving representation continue to be an interesting research topic? How do they make each of us a unique observer and interpreter of reality, adding quality to the creative design process? This book delves into the relationship between representation and landscape design to question how it can help us understand natural phenomena and support education in promoting the conscious use of visual languages. Contemporary landscape design refers to a complex set of elements. Representations simultaneously communicate multiple aspects and information: they manifest social needs, propose cultural models, report scientific data, and, last but not least, are a vehicle for expressiveness. Landscape design visualization has great potential, as it can take on diverse formulation modes. Today, it can make us think of the project as a hybrid and multiscalar process or a material and sensory experimentation, proving to be a great opportunity.

On the one hand, technologies have increased representation modes, thanks to the introduction of sophisticated systems. Digital programs make it possible to map vast territories with Geographic Information System (GIS) tools, create detailed three-dimensional models with Building Information Modeling (BIM), and interact with users through augmented reality or artificial intelligence (AI). On the other hand, there is a certain flattening of expressive languages - particularly in education - and the frequent reliance on repetitive and unoriginal styles in the representations produced. This can be found, in general, in contemporary society, which is characterized by continuous image consumption. No longer interested in spending time to know phenomenas, we tend to consume and sell. This demand leads designers to have to translate everything into rendering, almost compulsively. These are in demand everywhere: architecture, construction, and interior design. That is why this thesis refers to visual languages, understanding them both as a possibility for better project success and as an individual tool for expressing oneself consciously.

Some studios deal with post-production, digital visualization, and graphic communication, for which original research had been conducted, but more is desirable. Indeed, this case shows probably a certain distance between those who design and those who describe ideas. The propensity to entrust representation to visualisation professionals, typical in the current way of thinking about design to appear *à la page*, shows that perhaps this is not considered as a fundamental part of the creative process, that is, an opportunity to share information and formulate reasoning as unique and inimitable expressions. Many of the images produced then end up in magazines and, consequently, tend to spread a style that people repeat in a continuous cycle.

Various authors surmise that representation is experiencing a crisis, especially in education, as it would rarely be taught thoroughly as an expressive language. Many of them have rediscovered its importance as a complex cognitive system and recognize that drawing and manual representation allow irreplaceable intimacy and expressiveness. It seems necessary to understand how it can be preserved in today's design education, dealing with incredible technological innovations on the one hand and complex environmental challenges on the other. The aim of this reflection is primarily due to teaching methods. Indeed, the procedures adopted by most universities may explore more in-depth representation as art and as a visual language, as well as of colleagues of the academy of fine arts or the music conservatory are dedicated to artistic languages. This immediately suggests how students can meet the complexity of the creative process and visual language and its declinations.

Given that representing landscape design is a complex process, it is helpful to understand what references designers need to communicate effectively. Thus, in Chapter 1, the current need for representation in landscape design and the opportunities for hybridizing manual and digital drawing to contemplate and manage environmental transformations will be investigated. In Chapter 2, the historical relationship between representation and landscape design will be considered, starting from the anthropocentric model and arriving at the holistic model. Chapter 3 will focus on representation as a cognitive tool for developing students' critical and creative skills. Chapter 4 will analyze the role of representation in the European context to understand what forms creative processes can take. Finally, Chapter 5 will consider possible themes to overcome the homogenization of design languages.

We generally identify two meanings of the term "representation." One is material, that is, the depiction of the expression using images or plastic elements of aspects of reality or abstract concepts. The other meaning leads to a figuration comprehensible by the intellect. The derivation is philosophical; according to the meaning, "representation" is any process by which the content of perceptions, imaginations, and concepts presents itself to consciousness. Here, the term "representation" will be used to refer to creative processes in a broad sense, while "drawing" will be used whenever it proves necessary to focus on the technique of manual or digital drawing in a specific sense. Meanwhile, image selection is based on aspects like sensitivity, critical ability, and originality. These references are intended to highlight the legacy of artistic languages and the connection of the activity of landscape design with the fine arts. The same applies to literary texts and musical compositions, which can equally be considered forms of representation.

It is also necessary to clarify that the frequent references to art history and to the landscape's visual aspects are not intended to reduce the latter's concept to that of an image just in an aesthetic way. Conversely, it is intended to think about the process that leads to reflection through representation to understand and transform it. Anyone who has tried to draw a landscape, a face, or an animal extemporaneously knows that, in drawing it, we see things we were previously unaware of as if we begin to look at the world for the first time. This research will focus on the creative experience. This is a necessary discourse if the expressive languages of the project are to be enhanced.

Therefore, all references related to landscape representation — especially to painting — can be understood in this sense: that is, as an attempt to grasp, somewhat like the title of a well-known book by Konrad Lorenz, *Die Rückseite des Spiegels,* the other side of the mirror. If the mirror, for Lorenz, represents the human being reflecting what he knows with his senses, the other side of the mirror is everything that brings him to know the real world. The research is not intended to be exhaustive but to offer insights in considering representation in a new way in design and education. The goal was to recall the passion aroused by specific themes, reminding us how vast and surprising they can be. If, in our world, we communicate mainly through images, representation becomes an essential tool for effectively elaborating and communicating landscape design, understanding with an awareness of the needs related to the quality of life in our cities and on this planet. It is an opportunity to interpret the world and its phenomena, on which our way of seeing and thinking depends, thus our attitude toward landscape values and our approach to the transformations of nature.

CHAPTER ONE

Interpreting a World in Transformation

Representation has been practiced since Leonardo da Vinci's time to conduct empirical studies and gain a scientific understanding of natural processes.[1] By serving as a bridge between ideas and reality, representation has made possible the methodology that defines modern design attitudes. At the same time, perspective was one method used in science to depict volume and space. Perspective arose during the Renaissance from the necessity for logical rigour in exploring Euclidean space, a need generated primarily by the widespread optimism among artists of the 15th century that they could imitate nature. Today, the relationships woven between man and nature have taken unprecedented forms, become more complex, and seem destined for continuous evolution. A discovery of the last century is the idea that the universe in which we live is a phenomenon that includes multiple dimensions despite our experience being relegated to three spatial dimensions. When the theory of relativity was developed, we started to consider a fourth dimension, time, inseparable from the three spatial dimensions. Time also had to have a scale, so a four-dimensional metric for space-time was developed. For instance, if our geo-localization systems did not consider the time dilation caused by Earth's gravity in orbit, they would make errors on the order of metres.[2]

Suppose that perspective was the revolution of modernity that enabled us to scientifically define the laws of representation. We might be similarly interested in understanding how to compare multiple dimensions and integrate different disciplines into representation using visuals. The key idea is that natural events are multidimensional and multiscalar in their complexity, or at least they can be interpreted that way. We are prompted to investigate the role representation plays in imagining new relationships with the natural environment, considering the needs felt on a planetary and multidisciplinary level. New ways of investigating and understanding our relationship with space, society, and the environment are emerging in various disciplines. For example, physics is looking for a theory unifying general relativity and quantum mechanics, the former applicable to the universe and the latter to the microscopic scale, going so far as to conceive of the existence of strings and other dimensions, curved or rolled in on themselves.[3] Also, neuroscience is becoming interested in mirror neuron processes and possible relationships with empathy, and the philosophy of information is beginning to investigate the social role of the infosphere.[4,5] This ferment leads us to explore novel and complex connections between us and natural phenomena and, as one can imagine, significantly influences landscape design.

Landscape designers frequently have to lean toward a perspective that takes phenomena as a whole rather than concentrating on particular parts to deal with social, geopolitical, climatic, and environmental changes. There are other design ramifications to this strategy, which we may refer to as holistic. One is the requirement to comprehend and control intricate processes at all scales, including ecological ones. Another is moving past an abstract model-based design perspective and referring to transdisciplinary design, which prioritizes social welfare and quality of life while focusing on communities in an open and inclusive vision of society. How does a changing world regard artistic and aesthetic values is becoming an interesting question, as well as what modalities become necessary to represent projects in studios and universities.

Representation faces new processes, trying to meet unexpected needs that it can be considered. As Susan Ballard writes in *Art and Nature in the Anthropocene: Planetary Aesthetics*, the world we share is more than an Earth system: it is a planet both damaged and cherished, cared for and undermined by a dominant species. Parallel to science, art reflects this understanding of humanity's place in the world and the universe. This also entails significant implications in visual languages, allowing us to rethink, in some ways, the values we ascribe to nature and reshape its complex systems.[6,7] A particular way of seeing the Earth, namely its spherical depiction from space, inspired the inclination toward environmental protection. With the new images of the globe from orbit in the 1960s, people first began to think of the Earth as a predominantly blue sphere because of the vast expanse of its seas. This began to give it a vital, fascinating, and entirely unexpected character, which brought more significant interest in its natural aspects in those years.[8]

What seems to arouse greater interest is to conceive of the world and its transformations in a complex and articulated way, seeking to understand the connections between the parts more than the specifics and gain elasticity in dealing with leaps of scale, questioning unseen physical and mental processes. This kind of visual experimentation is found, for instance, in Richard Weller's *Atlas for the End of the World*, which is marked by a vision that considers the overall geopolitical situation of the Earth system.[9] As a landscape architect, Weller believes that humans have an opportunity to redesign and green the Earth, stabilize its climate, and protect the natural world. He reminds Abraham Ortelius atlas, made in Antwerp in the 16th century, as inspiration for mapping today's "end" of the world. Both ecological and cultural diversity are read in Weller's cartographies, bringing the concept of landscape representation to a transdisciplinary level. In this way, one understands the complexity of landscape design, sometimes with amusement and curiosity but always with a wide range of scientific and cultural issues to consider.

We can count on three-dimensional reconstructions of our galaxy are being made, allowing one to "jump" from a nearby star and know its most relevant information (Janelia Research Campus). Detailed three-dimensional reconstructions of neuronal maps are even starting to be made, making it possible to map these structures in the brain of a *Drosophila melanogaster*, or fruit fly, with precision to the nearest 20 μm (Stimulation Curriculum). The urge to depict life in all forms with amazement and curiosity appears fundamental to the need to depict the complexity of natural occurrences. The beautiful ultraviolet images of Venus published in *Nature* in 2020, for instance, which could show the presence of phosphine in the planet's atmosphere as a possible biological signature, have been much talked about and are still being studied.[10]

Still, a recent paper published in Science by Elizabeth Pennisi, "Getting the Big Picture of Biodiversity", shows the results of some research studying the health of biomes using satellites.[11] These can collect increasingly detailed spectrometric data on vegetation; they can measure, for example, photosynthetic activity by comparing the fluorescence of leaves based on specific emitted wavelengths. Michael Schaepman of the University of Zurich (UZH) has developed realistic models that analyze the productivity of a forest based on the change in biomass and the biochemical composition of plants. Satellite data can highlight, in this way, an enormous amount of information, including microbial activities and soil nutrient cycles.

The frontiers of science become relevant when describing very complex situations. The analogy lies in the fact that other dimensions are needed to describe a phenomenon at the quantum scale; for example, representational techniques can ideally draw inspiration from such models, which describe reality in an approach that sees beyond just its three-dimensional physical configuration but which are "projected" and thus carried over to the two-dimensional surface. Digital media enable managing an ever-increasing amount of data. Consequently, the creative process becomes multiscalar, with articulated connections, taking the observer from small to large dimensions and vice versa. It seems that even representational techniques determine our possibilities to handle natural phenomena and our aesthetic taste in conceiving and transforming spaces, in which the evolution of representational media and new aspirations influence each other.

We no longer have a sheet of paper to conceive landscape transformations but use mathematically unlimited point clouds and spaces, as in the case of vector programs: the possibilities of conceiving spaces increase exponentially. With this in mind, the creative process becomes elastic, taking us from large to small scale thanks to the structures of vector programs that allow such use. Christophe Girot works with highly complex software that can process vast amounts of data.[12] He builds intricate point clouds that let him map and examine terrain and landscape using specialized scanners coupled with drones. Numerous degrees of reading are available to the user depending on the vast amount of information acquired in his renders, including geography, topography, infrastructure, and land quality, to mention a few. The point clouds and mathematically infinite spaces of software thus offer multiple possibilities for managing the environment and conceiving its transformations, just as using easily interchangeable layers allows exchanges between languages, promoting new styles.[13]

The morphogenetic processes of the city and landscapes as the outcome of cause-and-effect nexuses can be understood only as multiscalar and multidimensional phenomena, and knowledge of the territory necessitates an understanding of the relationships between flows, areas, and networks. With the belief that multiscalarity is an interpretive lens of urban phenomena and, therefore, an unavoidable reference for rethinking contemporary urban design, Michelangelo Russo offers a reflection on the notion of scale to innovate disciplinary relations between architecture and planning in multiscalarity, dimensions, and spaces of contemporaneity. He contends that scale is unavoidable when interpreting and depicting things in a hierarchical or interrelated connection: "Multiscalarity, for example, is the distinctive character of the ecological dimension of environmental phenomena and represents a current interpretative category for dealing with the complexity of urban and territorial phenomena [...] as an inescapable value system for contemporary spatial design".[14] Integrating aesthetic and scientific languages and adding cultural and technical information proves possible. Multiple reading levels add value to the project, helping us conceive of the landscape more complexly and articulately. They also allow us to unveil its hidden dimensions, highlight its intrinsic relationships, and eviscerate its most essential values.

Science and technology prove to be an inexhaustible source of inspiration, even for those applying themselves to more creative disciplines. Precisely because of this, however, we maybe need to be aware of what we are doing and trying to achieve. While it is true that representation expresses itself in varied and complex forms, it seems essential to find points of reference allowing those who design to feel directed and inspired, preventing them from falling back into the flat application of available techniques. Indeed, considering the homogeneity found among designers' work, the risk of expressing oneself flatly and superficially is to be considered and is a critical issue not to be underestimated.

In the article "Planet Photoshop," Richard Weller expresses worry about the similarity of landscape depiction in many students' portfolios. He notes a certain monotony in the expressive languages embraced by the project.[15] According to Weller, the similarities between the different Photoshop-produced photographs show how current landscape aesthetics, originality, and individuality require greater criticality. He has dwelt on these aspects several times in his research, and in a recent article, he writes that the hyperrealism of the images used by landscape architecture offices gives clients a sense of confidence and comfort in the world they and the designers are aiming to create. Seemingly nice-looking, these images can, however, serve to disguise the deeper, structural ecological and social problems facing contemporary cities and reinforce landscape aesthetics as exclusively picturesque. Contrary to this, today, in universities, students and professors are trying to visualize landscape not as scenic but as complex processes. The interest in visualizing flows beyond the scenic frame is height-ended and made necessary by the overarching crisis of the Anthropocene.[16]

His words about hyperrealism in project representations ring tremendously accurate. The digital, so useful in some ways, has allowed us to settle into this tendency and to escape, through special effects, authentic dialogue with the users of the images. The dialogue between those who produce and receive images could be more communicative. Moreover, the problem with the hyperrealistic images that are so often resorted to is that, paradoxically, they are unreal. They are far removed from the reality we experience and distract from the actual communicative needs of representation. Many images seek to impress by showing idyllic visions of the project rather than consciously expressing ideas or emotions. They often tend to erase all traces of what they dislike to fill the void with some effect, perhaps depicting an urban "jungle". As an element that forms an essential part of the design, appropriate and targeted visual education could instead lead to even original, more innovative, and different elaborations.

In the past, representation generally comprised a series of hypotheses presented through elaborations that abstracted the object in question, highlighting only certain technical aspects. There was no need for the work to be understood by a broad audience, as the target audience was technicians or experts. Today, partly because of the issues related to the theme of participation, which is highly felt and requires expressions that are accessible to all, more and more simplification is being used, producing images that are perhaps more engaging but which do not then always have a direct match with reality. On the one hand, it turns out to be necessary "to be able to see," as Franco Zagari writes, and on the other, to acquire new languages suited to represent the complex phenomena that affect the landscape involving large population segments.[17] However, how do we formulate them?

James Corner states that a representation of landscape architecture is part of a generative activity that goes beyond analysis and drawing itself. Drawing is an "agent" that evokes the landscape, and the relationship between each sign and the actual landscape is unique every time. Therefore, it is essential to know how to communicate the qualities through the most appropriate media, techniques, and styles to evoke a rational and emotional sense that attracts and engages viewers.[18] An opportunity could be to use a greater variety of techniques, perhaps by recovering hand drawing, in search of new visual languages. Indeed, in the many forms it takes, the digital world can increase the use of manual drawing. Among others, one possibility for students and designers is to restart using manual techniques by combining them with digital ones to increase the transmissibility of ideas expressively and effectively. Various researchers, such as Nadia Amoroso, are investigating these opportunities - therefore, we will return to them later.

Some phrases from the preface to her book, *Representing Landscapes: Hybrid*, are illustrative: "Digital technology advances have transformed the design process over the last 40 years and offered designers powerful and exciting new tools to develop, edit, and evolve their design work. [...] Additionally, three-dimensional software capabilities advance the design of complex forms from conceptualization through fabrication. This has offered landscape architects and architects new processes to develop, construct, and communicate design ideas. However, with these advances, there has also been a loss. [...] a purely digital process can rob the final spatial experience of incredible landscapes' richness and humanity without integrating analogue methods".[19]

Despite the great potential of new technological frontiers, the question of what representation means for our design practice remains open. That is why artistic languages, which underlie representation, have relevance even in more professional areas such as landscape architecture. To understand this, we need only look at where the discipline comes from, how much it has in common with the fine arts, and how it conceives of the creative process by which to transform nature. Visualization is maybe not the final, formal product of the project, but rather the creative flow that feeds it. Connecting with this flow requires a conscious practice learned as the arts are learned in the art academy, in which design choices correspond to methods based on aesthetic principles, however different they may be. Technological productions, to become genuinely effective, but more importantly, meaningful, seem to need support from more creative skills, such as manual and artistic ones. The integration of both of these approaches is the necessary stimulus for progress in this field. Therefore, if new needs emerge in landscape design, as noted, there is also the possibility of formulating new languages through multiple combinations. It thus proves necessary to delve into the topic of visual languages to understand how they can help us conceive transformations with their complexities.

NOTES

[1] L. Geddes, *Watermarks: Leonardo Da Vinci and the Mastery of Nature*. (Princenton University Press, 2020).

[2] S. W. Hawking, *A Brief History of Time*, 2005.

[3] L. Randall, *Warped Passages: Unravelling the Universe's Hidden Dimensions*. (London: Penguin, 2006).

[4] G. Rizzolatti, A. Gnoli, *In te mi specchio. Per una scienza dell'empatia*. (Milan: Rizzoli, 2016).

[5] L. Floridi, Infosfera. *Etica e filosofia nell'età dell'informazione*. (Turin: Giappichelli, 2009).

[6] The reference of the concept of Anthropocene is first expressed in P. J. Crutzen, *Earth System Science in the Anthropocene*. (Berlin: Springer, 2006), 13-18.

[7] S. Ballard, *Art and Nature in the Anthtopocene: Planetary Aesthetics*. (London: Routledge, 2021), 10-14.

[8] D. Nardo, *The Blue Marble: How a Photograph Revealed Earth's Fragile Beauty*. (Mankato: Capstone, 2014), 4-13.

[9] R. J. Weller, C. Hoch and C. Huang, *Atlas for the End of the World*. (Philadelphia: University of Pennsylvania Press, 2017).

[10] J. O'Callaghan, "Life on Venus? Scientists hunt for the truth", *Nature* 586, no. 7828 (2020): 182-183. From more recent studies seem not to be phosphine.

[11] E. Pennisi, "Getting the Big Picture of Biodiversity", *Science* 374, no. 6570 (November 19, 2021): 926-931.

[12] C. Girot, "The Elegance of Topology", *Landscript* 3 (2013): 79-116.

[13] J. Walliss, "Landscape architecture and the digital turn: Towards a productive critique", *Journal of Landscape Architecture* 13, no. 3 (2018): 12-15.

[14] M. Russo, "Multiscalarità: dimensioni e spazi della contemporaneità", *Archivio di Studi Urbani e Regionali,* XLVI, no. 113 (2015): 5-22. The paragraph has been here translated by the author, D.S.

[15] R. Weller, J. Ho, "Planet Photoshop", in *Landscape Architecture*, 4 (2015): 4.

[16] R. Weller, "The Hype of Representation: Some Thoughts on the Roles of the Hyperreal and the Hyperobject in Contemporary Landscape Architecture," *Ri-Vista. Research for landscape architecture* 19, no. 2 (2020): 30-39.

[17] F. Zagari, *Sul paesaggio: Lettera aperta* (Melfi: Libria 2013), 104-112.

[18] J. Corner, "Representation and landscape", *Word & Image*, 8, no. 3 (1992): 243-275.

[19] K. Mikyoung, "Introduction" in *Representing Landscapes: Hybrid.* ed. N. Amoroso (London: Routledge 2016), XI.

CHAPTER TWO

Landscape, Garden, Art: A Holistic Perspective

An aspect to consider is the historical background that links the landscape project to representation. This can lead us to understand how aesthetic values have brought us closer to thinking about natural ones and landscape design. In a well-known book from the last century, *Landscape into Art*, Kenneth Clark already suggested that how we relate to nature depends, in some ways, on how we represent it. He argues that landscape painting, in particular, highlights the stages through which this relationship has evolved.[1] This concept makes us think of representation as a medium that intermediates and explicates the values we attach to natural phenomena. This relationship is inherent not only in the correlation between man-made artifacts and natural elements but also in its recognizability by a subject, a group, or a population. The point of view that generates it has its basis in the aesthetic roots, which begin to consolidate from the Renaissance when the perspective framework puts the subject-observer at the center of the natural phenomena. The same landscape begins to assume dignity as the subject of pictorial representation, which previously saw it only as the background of historical or religious subjects. However, it would be incorrect to limit the concept of landscape to that of an image; on the contrary, image and representation allow us to read and interpret it, enhance it, and change it through design. In 2000, the European Landscape Convention of Florence stated that "'Landscape' designates a certain part of the territory, as perceived by people, whose character results from the action of natural and/or human factors and their interrelationships."[2] This seemingly simple concept is exemplified in a "formula" suggested by Mikael Jakob in *The Landscape*, according to which the landscape is based on a relationship that can be called "Subject + Nature."[3]

One of the many aspects of the concept of landscape refers to visual reasoning, and this is not reductive to other values, such as ecological and social ones. In *Paesaggi, Forme, Immagini,* Rossella Salerno reminds us that "landscape represents itself visually, through certain forms, images of the way a society perceives and expresses the vision of its environmental context."[4] In *Filosofia del Paesaggio*, Paolo D'Angelo points out that we experience a more complex nature than a purely sensory one when we view a landscape. Our experience organizes what we see based on imaginative, emotional, memorial, and identifying components.[5] Many philosophers have highlighted the cultural connection with art. For example, concerning the aesthetic experience of landscape, Emily Brady argues that it is primarily about perceptual and imaginative values. Perception and imagination underlie the appreciation of nature on sources familiar to aesthetics. By providing this framework, aesthetic value can be recognised as distinct from other environmental values, such as ecological value.[6] In *Brief Treatise on Landscape*, Alan Roger believes that the origin of the landscape is artistic and that an area becomes a landscape when it is represented artistically.[7] Ernst Gombrich formulates a similar thought in *The Theory of Art in the Renaissance and the Origin of Landscape*, where he states that it is not art inspired by nature but painting that teaches us what to see in it.[8] Indeed, some go so far as to deem a landscape worthy of consideration only because painters have taught us to regard it as such, going so far as to reach the paradox of Oscar Wilde, who wrote that "Nature imitates what the work of art proposes to it."[9]

The painting indeed formed the aesthetic assumptions of cultural interest in landscape. In this regard, as Rossella Salerno writes, it is helpful to reflect on two phenomena that appear at the beginning of modernity: the emergence of the Renaissance perspective and the emergence of landscape as an object of pictorial representation. In both cases, the natural world is brought back to the centrality of an individual who has become the benchmark of everything.[10] As much as it allows us to admire the beauty of nature through its image, the perspective device is an instrument of design through which the world and, thus, the landscape takes shape.

Landscape representation has a long tradition, born before the development of perspective. Franco Panzini, an historian of landscape and garden history, shows us that one of the earliest representations of a garden is the Egyptian tomb of Nebamun, dating from around 1350 B.C.E., depicting a rectangular body of water surrounded by papyrus, date palms, fig trees, and sycamores. Images of natural scenes and gardens were also depicted in ancient Rome. The most notable case is undoubtedly the Villa of Livia Drusilla, consort of Augustus, built between 30 and 25 B.C.E.[11] In the Near East, depictions of Persian gardens are known from the school of illuminated painting in Tabriz, a city particularly rich in gardens; for this reason, it is even mentioned by Marco Polo in *The Million*. He recalls that Tabriz artists took to depicting the events narrated by certain manuscripts, setting them in formal gardens or natural landscapes, thus going so far as to illuminate the *Shāh-Nāmeh* ("Book of Kings") written by the poet Ferdowsi around 1000 C.E.[12] In the Western Middle Ages, the few representations of gardens produced appear to be primarily related to the creation of monastic gardens until the emergence of an accurate idea of landscape based on the harmony of the colonized and productive countryside, culminating in Ambrogio Lorenzetti's well-known cycle of frescoes, *Allegory and Effects of Good and Bad Government*, in which workers tending the land and animals emerge among other elements. In the East, in the same period, garden culture was deeply influenced by landscape painting. China, in particular, was devoted todepicting scenic aspects of the Chinese landscape, such as mountainous environments, hills, rivers, and waterfalls, in a symbiotic development.[13]

In the Renaissance, representations of landscapes and gardens also began to determine new land arrangements. These took shape from the creation of villas, in which an attempt was made to give order to nature. Examples of representations include Giusto Utens images of the Medici villas around Florence. Panzini wrote that in the 17th century, with unprecedented scale and complexity, the designs for new villas, especially French ones, had to be accompanied by detailed executive plans. It was essential to survey the conformation of the land and the water network with precise measurements, plans, and sections and the new project elevations, regularizing the configuration thanks to terraces, slopes, and so on.[14] Throughout Europe, the creation of new gardens was made possible by the development of surveying techniques, allowing significant transformations of natural environments. Interest in the cartographic representation of the land grew enormously because of the spatial changes required due to natural phenomena, such as river floods and tides, in the Netherlands.

The achievements of significant land arrangements depended on advances in cartography and painting, which was considered an indispensable aesthetic orientation.[15] Many landscape painters in this period devoted themselves to painting and were, at the same time, capable artists. André Le Nôtre, in addition to studying geometry and architecture, delved into painting with Simon Vouet (1590–1649), Louis XIII's favorite painter. In 1643, Vouet became the draughtsman of the king's gardens, and a few years later, he was commissioned to create the castle of Vaux-le-Vicomte, working with the painter Charles Le Brun and the architect Luis Le Vau.[16] That pictorial sensibility influenced cultural interest in and aesthetic taste for modifications of natural environments is evident in the developments that landscape design had in England in the 18th century. William Kent began his journey by studying painting in Rome in the *atelier* of Benedetto Luti, an artist in the circle of Carlo Maratta. Many believe that, in Kent's interventions, the painter's gaze is even more significant than that of the architect, and it is curious to note that there are no plans or tables with precise measurements but only sketches and drawings, which look like preparatory studies for a painting.[17]

Humphry Repton, already accustomed to landscape painting, decided to employ his mastery of the visual arts as a design tool through the creation of the famous *Red Books*, each project is accompanied by an illustrated watercolour album, in which precise references to the site, before and after the intervention, are visible. Plans and drawings are always accompanied by two sheets overlaid by a tab, which highlights images of the site in its original layout and the one it would later assume.[18] The *Red Books* made by Repton are a valuable record of how representation gave way to new social needs, such as allowing customers to choose their preferred style. The titles of the texts are indicative: sketches, hints, observations, designs, and fragments (i.e., "sketches," "hints," "observations," "designs," and "considerations" about gardens). His projects aim to improve the landscape by reconfiguring natural and manufactured elements into a new whole.[19] In this way, Repton succeeds in foreshadowing through the medium of painting the future layout of the garden, predicting its final arrangement with what will be possible to see.[20]

Here there begins to be a significant breakthrough. In the aesthetics of the picturesque, the work of the landscape gardener becomes similar to that of the painter, as both have a similar attitude towards nature. Central to the training of the landscape gardeners is the close observation of nature, which will lead him to acquire an unlimited resource of field ideas. Landscape gardeners and painters draw from landscapes that are the most pleasing, the "laughing parts," to create a new whole - something beyond ordinary nature without ceasing to be natural.[21] This process implies a deep relationship with natural phenomena mediated by painterly taste. Recall, for example, William Gilpin's writing, *Three Essays: On Picturesque Beauty, on Picturesque Travel, and on Sketching Landscape.*[22] In the last essay, Gilpin states that the picturesque traveller should master the art of sketching. To do this, he recommends the careful choice of viewpoint and definition of framing. He distinguishes between two types of sketching: the original made in charcoal, which serves only to recall the site to memory, and the sketch embellished to show acquaintances the places visited.

The picturesque traveller should, of course, employ the indispensable picturesque features of irregularities, *chiaroscuro* effects and free brushstrokes in the composition.[23] In addition, Gilpin recommends using the "Claude mirror," an invention that tradition attributes to Claude Lorrain. This slight convex, blackened mirror reflects glimpses of landscapes (a handcrafted wide-angle lens!), which becomes an indispensable tool in the picturesque traveller's kit.[24]

An artist and author of a treatise on perspective, Pierre-Henri de Valenciennes, also devotes extensive space to the relationship between landscape, painting, and garden art. In his view, the latter is one of the fine arts, so it has a privileged relationship with painting. Between the landscape and the landscape painter, there exists, as Rossella Salerno points out, a *liaison si forte et si naturelle* articulated on the equal knowledge of three fundamental aspects: the characters of the landscape, the techniques in imitating nature, and the laws of perspective.[25] The artist-gardener approaches the landscape artist in using compositional techniques that require knowledge of the laws of perspective to order objects in proper proportion to prevent both fatigue and distraction of the eye. The attitude of the landscape gardner should be understood as a curious process aimed at understanding natural phenomena and their beauty to redefine one's relationship with them.

This was an attitude that involved several artistic disciplines at the same time. Musicians were interested in representing the landscape in that way. The music, called "descriptive," which was aimed at reproducing aspects of reality and nature, found its most significant expression in the symphonic and piano works of those times. For istance, Ludwig van Beethoven composed his Sixth Symphony describing rural landscapes, including peasant dances and the sudden arrival of a storm. The second generation of Romantics carried on that revolutionary attitude more systematically. Felix Mendelsohn first dedicated his Third Symphony to Scottish landscapes and the Fourth to Italian landscapes. With the same Romantic attitude, Robert Schumann wrote the Third Symphony to celebrate the majesty of the Rhine. Years later, descriptions of natural elements that were neither romantic nor realistic arose. Debussy adopted an impressionistic, pointillist, and decidedly analytical approach. A case in point is "La Mer", which he composed during a stay in Eastbourne on the coast of the English Channel, in which each note recreates an impression of a particular place.[26]

Gardens, anyway, require a special effort: standing and contemplating what nature manages to create in an enclosed space managed by humans. It is perhaps a further step in our short but lively journey: describing landscapes designed within a garden. In his *Années de Pèlerinage* for solo piano, Franz Liszt dedicated one piece to the cypresses of Villa d'Este and another to the aqueduct of the same villa. The first is structured on chords that evoke extremely introspective sonorities as if to paint a strong *chiaroscuro* of columnar evergreen trees. In the second, however, Liszt tries to evoke not only the sound but also the charm of the fountains of the Villa d'Este in Tivoli. Maurice Ravel, with "Le Jardin Féerique", brought the clean and bright "French" orchestral sound into the space of a garden instead. Manuel De Falla worked with the same intent to describe the atmospheres of gardens, and with his piano concerto "Noches en los Jardines de España", he takes us instead to an exotic world that evokes the non-European origin of gardens such as the Alhambra.

Poetry as a form of representation (and design) is also possible. In *The Figure in the Landscape*, John Dixon Hunt devotes interesting reflections to the relationship between poetry, painting, and garden art in the 18th century.[27] The number of poems, especially poems passionately written by influential English authors such as Alexander Pope, Horace Walpole, and James Thomson, to name a few, is remarkable and demonstrates how, parallel to painting, the intertwining of the garden and poetry was strong at the time when the culture of landscape design was created and consolidated. This can be summed up in Walpole's phrase, "Poetry, Painting, and Gardening, or the Science of Landscape, will forever by men of taste be deemed Three Sisters, or The Three New Graces who dress and adorn nature".[28]

Dixon Hunt recalls that some literary representations of the English garden inspired, along with painting, the ideal of the picturesque garden, emphasising the role of the painter-gardener. The most famous literary statement favouring natural gardens is in John Milton's description of Eden.[29] However, it is the poet Alexander Pope, in the Epistle to Lord Burlington, who sums up the equivalence that creating a garden is like painting a picture:

> *Consult the Genius of the place in all;*
> *that tells the water to rise or fall,*
> *or helps the ambitious hill that heav'ns to scale,*
> *or scoops in circling theatres the vale;*
> *calls in the country catch opening glades,*
> *joins willing Woods and varies shades from shade;*
> *now breaks, or now directs, intending lines,*
> *paint as you plant, and as you work, designs.*[30]

Pope's interest in gardens was so strong that it led him to formulate the famous equation "all gardening is landscape painting" and to think that the art of gardening is even older and closer to God's work than poetry. The cultural scenario of the art of gardens, with such interdisciplinary influences, seems predisposed to consider nature peculiarly, in which pictorial taste and botanical interest manifest as two parallel fields, as if they were complementary. The interest in the representation of nature is based on a new feeling towards its "vital" characters, and the creative desire to transform it reveals the search for a new relationship with it. More and more scientific aspects of natural science begin to be considered, giving rise to a remarkable symbiosis between artistic and scientific languages.

Alexander von Humboldt, for example, interpreted precisely through the representation of the new inclination towards ecology. He was the first to use pictorial language to understand ecological issues in the modern sense. Humboldt's famous profiles respond to the goal of representing the relationship and functioning of elements with each other, and his representations in mixed form section/profile propose a modern formulation of the concept of landscape. In the second half of the 19th century, Adolphe Alphand, in his numerous woodcuts elaborated for *Les Promenades de Paris*, began to make the representation a tool, at once pictorial and technical, to document the realisation of French parks, until it became a manifesto of the aesthetic and functional criteria of the modern city, where: "[...] the magnificent illustrations, plates of admirable graphic and technical quality, made by various artists, made it at once a product of art and a manual for the offices of the great municipalities and favoured the vast dissemination of the work".[31]

A similar inclination towards these aspects, but applied to the garden, can be found in Gertrude Jekyll, in the following century. Panzini writes that interest in painting and the fine arts was renewed more than ever. Not only did Jekyll study painting, but she also had relationships with the primary animators of the Arts and Crafts movement, such as John Ruskin and painters Edward Burne-Jones and Dante Gabriel Rossetti, who opposed the brutality of the Industrial Revolution. This interest was directed, in a highly original way, at the qualities of plants. Relying on her profound botanical knowledge and the refinement that came from her study of painting, Jekyll invented mixed borders, a style characterized by chromatic sequences obtained through the skillful juxtaposition of native plants placed in a free and seemingly haphazard manner and which was destined to be a great success and attract numerous epigones.[32]

Botany and painting interested Roberto Burle Marx, who approached the study of art and botanical research with equal curiosity, using his abstract works as references for his design style. Seeking a close relationship with contemporary figurative art and using novel plant and mineral materials, Burle Marx not only ably complemented his country's modern architects but also embodied the spirit of the times in his campaigns against deforestation and in defence of the environment.[33] Moreover, many landscape architects became interested in including more expressive language to communicate the intent of the design, which was increasingly seen as a complex system that was not reducible to the mere sum of its parts. At the time when Ian McHarg published *Design with Nature*, we find the same attention to ecological issues in Italy in the work of Cesare Leonardi and Franca Stagi, who, in addition to publishing *L'architettura degli alberi* (a volume that had a significant influence in the discipline of landscape architecture in Italy) gave representation and ecology a very prominent role in their projects (as in the case of the *Parco della Resistenza* in Modena in 1969) through drawings that deliberately drew on avant-garde techniques.[34]

This becomes particularly evident, in a certain leap forward, in the drawings of the OMA group. In the drawings for the 1983 Parc de la Villette, the articulation of the project into bands and the further subdivision of each band into places for diversified activities is represented in an entirely new way. This project organized the dynamic coexistence of some activities by parallel bands and regulated their mutual interaction. If we look at images that Nadia Amoroso selected in *Digital Landscape Now*, it is surprising how consolidated this vision has become.[35] This is evident in how figures tend to dematerialize in a continuous search for the fusion of forms. It also has much of the pictorial legacy of previous centuries. Trees become patches of color, combined with pieces of photographs, kneaded with effects and the play of light – as if somehow, through the project, we wish to merge with nature again. The exact process can be found in musical languages. It is curious that the arpeggios in C-sharp major of Franz Liszt's "Les jeux d'eau à la Villa d'Este", for example, which denoted his enchanted gaze at the beauty of the garden, have now become chromatic scales in quintiles, sexting and settings superimposed on each other, like incessant waves if one looks at the score of "Become Ocean" by John Luther Adams. The composition, for which Adams won the Pulitzer Prize in 2014, with a similar scale of contemporary representations, celebrates through innovative musical languages the life that has emerged from the sea at a time when, as the ice melts, we may once again become ocean.[36]

We arrive at the question of what directions can be taken in the search for quality and innovation in visualization. From a cultural - historical point of view, it is interesting that landscape representation, moving towards a holistic approach, lives to a revival of the artist-gardener in project culture. Noël van Dooren cites the case of the Maaskant Award, which was given to garden architect Piet Oudolf in December 2014. Landscape historian Erik de Jong, who was asked to read the *laudatio* on that occasion, argues that the choice is significant because it demonstrates the emancipation of landscape architecture. Also, since he is typically a nurseryman and garden designer, Oudolf "is not an architectural designer who conceives design mainly in terms of space, line, function and mass, as was customary in the modernist tradition in the second half of the 20th century." He says this makes us rediscover a substantial tradition of 20th-century garden and landscape art that we had forgotten.[37]

People such as Oudolf, Dan Pearson, and Nigel Dunnet seem to keep alive the spirit of the landscape artist who is an outsider to the great ateliers and who lives the creative process with freedom and independence – with the possibility of connecting with the artistic field (in this, the New Perennials are somewhat reminiscent of the New Arcadians, such as Ian Hamilton Finlay and Charles Jencks).[38] The gardening artist's figure is alive, but in a contemporary guise, it seems promising. The possibility that the holistic view of the discipline of landscape architecture gives us is also crucial in terms of representation. The fact that the discipline began as a sister to the fine arts thus allows us not to forget the potential that the aesthetic (not aestheticizing) aspect has in the creative practice it implies. This practice, the creative process, is a field of ferment in which ideas materialize and works are born.

This idea of representation is essentially artistic. The landscape discipline, rooted in the Beaux Arts, shows an extrordinary human side of creativity. That is the place in which we can regain interest and feeling alive as designers. Instead, the conduit can be university education, which can nurture this by accompanying students and young professionals in realizing the full creative potential of landscape design. Visualization, in its most unrestricted and original forms, is once again becoming that essential means of mediating our relationship with natural phenomena, maybe a way of being landscape architects, gardeners, and artists simultaneously. What is certain is that Pope's motto, "Paint as you plant," leads us today, as Weller also does in a recent lecture in Florence for the Italian Scientific Society of Landscape Architecture in 2018 to talk about "designing" the planet.[39]

NOTES

[1] K. Clark, *Landscape into Art*. (Edinburgh: Pellican Books, 1949), 17.

[2] "Chapter 1," in *Proceedings of the European Landscape Convention*, Florence, Italy, 2000.

[3] M. Jakob, *Il paesaggio* (Bologna: Il Mulino, 2009), 30-55.

[4] R. Salerno, *Paesaggi Forme Immagini* (Milano: Libreria Clup, 2006), 9.

[5] P. D'Angelo, *Filosofia del paesaggio* (Macerata: Quodlibet, 2010), 13.

[6] *Ibidem*, 109.

[7] *Ibidem*, 17.

[8] *Ibidem*, 18.

[9] S. Santuccio, *Note sul paesaggio: esplorazione antologica tra paesaggio e disegno*. (Rome: Tab, 2021), 38-40. Wilde wrote that in *The Decay of Lying* (1889-1891).

[10] R. Salerno, *Paesaggi Forme Immagini*, 18-19.

[11] F. Panzini, *Progettare la natura. Architettura del paesaggio e dei giardini dalle origini all'epoca contemporanea*. (Bologna: Zanichelli, 2005), 45.

[12] *Ibidem*, 67.

[13] *Ibidem*, 184.

[14] *Ibidem*, 137.

[15] S. Heyde S. "The French Picturesque and the Invention of Landscape Architecture as a Design Discipline," *Journal of Landscape Architecture* 12, no. 3 (2017): 76-87.

[16] F. Panzini, *Progettare la natura. Architettura del paesaggio e dei giardini dalle origini all'epoca contemporanea*, 151-153. The same can be said of the painter Hubert Robert, who participated in the realisation of the park for Russeau in Ermenonville and helped to define the aesthetic orientation of the project, as Heyde also recalls.

[17] H. Walpole, *History of Modern Taste in Gardening*, ed. by J.D. Hunt (New York: Ursus, 1995), 38.

[18] T. Calvano, *Viaggio nel pittoresco: Il giardino inglese fra arte e natura* (Rome: Donzelli Editore, 1996), 88.

[19] *Ibidem*, 88.

[20] Salerno, *Paesaggi Forme Immagini*, 95.

[21] *Ibidem*, 95.

[22] W. Gilpin, *Three Essays on Picturesque Beauty, on Picturesque Travel and on Sketching Landscape* (London, 1794).

[23] The concept of the picturesque traveller is in this case complementary to that of the landscape gardener.

[24] Calvano, *Viaggio nel pittoresco: Il giardino inglese fra arte e natura*, 126.

[25] R. Salerno, *Paesaggi Forme Immagini*, 43.

[26] G. Manzoni, *Guida all'ascolto della musica sinfonica*, (Milan: Mondadori, 2014), 43-45, 279-280, 399-400.

[27] J. D. Hunt, *The Figure in the Landscape: Poetry, Painting and Gardening during Eighteenth Century* (Baltimore: John Hopkins University Press, 1989).

[28] *Ibidem*, I.

[29] *Ibidem*, 55-56.

[30] *Ibidem*, 77. In the poem, the words "paint as you plant" stand out.

[31] Panzini, *Progettare la natura*, 257-258.

[32] *Ibidem*, 295-296.

[33] M. Barbiero, "Roberto Burle Marx, architetto paesaggista, o giardiniere, come egli spiritosamente ama definirsi," *Rosanova* 36 (2014): 30-59.

[34] A. Metta, *Paesaggi d'autore: il Novecento in 120 progetti* (Firenze: Alinea, 2008), 138-139.

[35] N. Amoroso, *Digital Landscape Architecture Now* (London: Thames & Hudson, 2012).

[36] The composition was commissioned by the Seattle Symphony Orchestra in 2013.

[37] N. van Dooren, "Drawing Time: The Representation of Growth, Change and Dynamics in Dutch Landscape Architectural Practice after 1985," PhD diss. (Academy of Architecture Amsterdam, 2017), 161-162.

[38] New Arcadian are a movement that started in the 1980s in the United Kingdom that makes use of experimental artistic languages in gardens.

[39] Reference is made to the *Lectio Magistralis* "Designing a Planet" by Richard Weller for the Italian Scientific Society of Landscape Architecture - IASLA, Florence, Italy, November 26, 2018.

CHAPTER THREE

The Visual Languages and the Project

The current practice of landscape design implies the aknowledgment of a considerable amount of information. This points to a further type of needs to be kept in mind, namely the personal ones that invest communication and interaction between those who represent and those who receive information, as well as the ability to observe and reason critically. As Caroline Lavoie writes in *Sketching the Landscape: Exploring a Sense of Place*, "Drawing is just as much a response to our cultural identity. Thus, each drawing is a unique reconstruction of one's perception of space, a critical aspect of how one proceeds with visual research".[1] From here, we understand the centrality of visual language, mainly drawing, not only as a representation tool but also as communication and awareness. It is appropriate to shed light on the theories that have led to representation being considered a language worthy of study.

Ernst Gombrich reminds us that the distinction between what we see and what we induce through the intellect is ancient: Pliny (23–79 C.E.), for example, believed that the mind is the proper instrument of sight, while he attributed to the eyes the role of a vessel that collects and transmits information to consciousness; in his *Optics* (c. 150), Ptolemy recognized the importance of the function of judgment in the process of vision; Alhazen (d. 1038) inferred somewhat from his studies that nothing visible is understood by sight alone.[2] In the 18th century, for some time, scientific naturalism challenged this tradition; John Locke held that the eye reacted only to light and color, while George Berkeley, in *An Essay Towards a New Theory of Vision*, assumed that all our knowledge was attained exclusively through the senses. From the end of the next century, however, the emerging psychology of perception overcame the problem that first empiricism and then the emergence of optical physiology had posed. In *Über den Ursprung der künstlerischen Tätigkeit*, Konrad Fiedler suggested that even the simplest sense impression is a mental fact. While Maurice Merleau-Ponty published *Phenomenology of Perception*, James Jerome Gibson and Rudolf Arnheim wrote *The Perception of the Visual World* and *Art and Visual Perception*, respectively, which analyzed art and perception as complex mental and psychological phenomena.[3]

Later, various studies emerged on the psychology of perception, beginning with understanding the essential relationships between figure and background, between fullness and emptiness. In particular, the projective and interpretative faculty of forms on the part of the observer became of interest in the debate on perception, which allow him to recognize elements of the natural world based on what he already knows through experience.[4] These concepts, which are acquired in the theory of perception, make it possible to begin to consider the depth of relationships between observer and design and how complex they can be when translated into the ability to observe the real world. An example is the recent neuroscientific studies by Stine Vogt, Svein Magnussen, and Robert Solso on the relationship between painting, eye movement, and neural processes.[5,6] Howard Riley, a contemporary perception theorist, states that information is consolidated in the process of representation and that it fulfils the functions of a language. Perception of our environment is a prerequisite for moving within it and acting on it, as much as for reflecting on it and making sense of it to share it with others.[7] While Gilpin intuitively afforded a lot of importance to the skill of drawing, considering it on par with the skill of writing ("equally necessary to fix and communicate its respective ideas"), we today know that the visual language is so important because it involves a cognitive process that fulfils the functions of a language.

This milestone is extremely relevant. As Riley points out, until Gibson proposed his ecological approach to understanding visual perception, all theories were based on the assumption that retinas were passive receivers of light stimuli. These impulses would then be transformed into knowledge by a presumed innate ability to interpret the stimulus (nativist theory) or by a process of unconscious inference, matching the stimulation to previously stored experiences (empiricist theory).[8] He also notes that, because of these cultural influences, Gombrich's view — based on a mixture of nativist and empiricist ideas — is better known in art schools than Gibson's work.[9] Gombrich focuses on perception, which leads him to the idea that drawing is a record of perception as he writes. From studies that came after his, we know that drawing does not just record perceptions: an image does not just imitate seeing, what it records and consolidates is information, more then sensed data. This confirms drawing as a "semogenic" process. Drawing is similar to language, as it transforms the perception of materials into cultural values and converts matter into meaning. Regarding this concept, we quote Michael Halliday's words: "A language is a system of meanings, a semiotic system, to give it a technical name. But it is more than that; it is a system that makes meanings: it is not only semiotic but semogenic".[10] Drawing operates as a language. It is a language not only because it is a system of signs but also because it can create meaning through them. The same occurs in writing and reading a text. When we write, we generate a word made of signs and a meaning that can be understood by the intellect. Thus, a tangle of pencil marks may not only represent an accurate or abstract object but take on a meaning intelligible by the beholder's mind.

Consequently, the painting and the paper should not be considered two-dimensional replicas of reality but an opportunity for human beings to understand and shape something vast. Ásthildur Jónsdóttir suggests *tous court,* that "representation acts as a window that interprets the world," offering us a combination of critical and creative thinking.[11] Anyone who has tried to extemporaneously draw something – a face, a landscape – as mentioned above, knows that we understand things that were previously unknown as beginners that see the world anew, an awareness that is fundamental to forming designers who are interpreters of reality and use critical thinking. In this sense, the creative process of representation confronts us with the world as interpreters of its phenomena and no longer as spectators. At the same time, it connects us to others and allows us to be understood. It would need to be considered in education if we are to inspire proper processes for designers to become conscious interpreters of their time.

It is interesting to recognize a mirroring of the finest emotional and intellectual qualities in representation. The process it implies allows for the intimate expression that arises from self-reflection, which should be enough to make us consider representation with an eye towards it. Let us dwell specifically now on the qualities of drawing, understood as a manual practice. If we are dealing with a language, teaching should educate us to understand and use it, starting with knowing the techniques by which it takes shape. However, the idea that drawing is something automatic or subordinate is seen quite often. We hear many people say with conviction that they cannot draw. Nevertheless, it has been shown that in normal conditions, almost everyone can do it satisfactorily when they learn to "see" and "reason" correctly in spatial terms.[12] It means that even today, unfortunately, many students have to learn to draw on their own, empirically and with effort.

Relevant to this perspective is the research conducted by Angela Brew, Andrea Kantrowitz, and Michelle Fava in "Drawing Connections: New Directions in Drawing and Cognition Research" on how much our understanding of the connections between drawing and intellectual abilities is developing. They report on research activity related to the "Thinking Through Drawing" symposium, showing the substantial relevance of visual education in our time. What emerges is that the growing understanding of the cognitive function of drawing is producing relevant results in many areas, such as in the development of general mental skills in education.[13] This is important as less attention is being given to such processes and visual education today. In "A Decline in Drawing Ability?", Michelle Fava points out that teaching methods have changed significantly in recent years. Research shows that drawing skills are less relevant in the United Kingdom (the survey area).

Drawing as a means of representation and communication remains valued but many times is not considered essential. That is, drawing to facilitate the thinking process is increasingly recognized as a skill that brings innovation but is rarely taught. Many teachers fear that the skills underlying this process are being increasingly left out. Fava's study, therefore, frames the problem as an imbalance between the creative process and creative outcomes. Indeed, in teaching methods, value should be placed on drawing as a process that enables young people to work creatively and productively.[14] Given the theoretical advances that allow for a greater understanding over time of the emotional qualities associated with drawing, Fava again calls for a rediscussion of the role of drawing in art and design curricula in "What is the Role of Observational Drawing in contemporary art and design curricula?". This re-discussion would place a renewed emphasis on drawing's importance as a process and way to make teaching more stimulating, especially in university settings.[15] These are just some recent studies that indicate the current design research trend. Representation has a prominent role in education and could have a greater weight in universities. Therefore, it is necessary to refrain from settling for the marginal role given to studying visual languages in education at all levels. It is essential to emphasize and explore the possibilities of representation as a creative process.

Returning to the landscape project, it is clear that drawing allows for critical thinking about countless aspects of reality and reading the territory and its palimpsest. Moreover, as an intermediary extension between reality and consciousness, it allows for imagining future scenarios not yet defined. The process leads the planner to understand and interpret phenomena to give them new meaning and communicate them to society, like the cases discussed in the previous chapter. In other words, as Caroline Lavoie always reminds us, design generates awareness: "Drawing in the landscape creates an awareness of the place, a distinct form of information gathering and understanding of the landscape setting. [...] The act of awareness in drawing involves our imaginative perception of space, as reflected in our cultural identity and with our physical senses. For instance, the perception of space, how we frame a view, and how we define its boundaries are critical dimensions in design".[16]

The choices in this creative process manifest the designer's criterion and strategies adopted in the design. In designing, he chooses a point of view and a method. In each representation, we can glimpse his thinking. Through drawing, an idea is manifested, which in turn expresses the degree of authenticity and quality of the project. Daniela Colafranceschi has effectively summarized this aspect, "We have many graphic, photographic, and digital means today to compose. Drawing is no longer the indispensable tool of an expressive language if it is not an option. This 'option' differentiates between a drawing to reproduce and a drawing that becomes a language and a storytelling tool."[17] Drawing becomes the "option" that makes the difference. It proves necessary to recover the role of manual drawing, which guarantees this intelligent and empathetic approach to representation. In that case, an opportunity is provided to use styles with a certain degree of abstraction, such as cartooning. Again, a further opportunity lies in combining manual and digital techniques.

Representations that we can call "hybrid" allow for the same mode of interaction as in manual drawing, a cognitive tool that unites hands and minds while disposing of the innovations provided by the digital world. The exciting aspect of mixed technique representations is that they emphasize drawing as an expressive tool and a language applied to landscape phenomena. In this regard, the words of Paul Russell and Martin Holland are adequate: "While it is tempting to regard mixed media containing digital and analogue sources to represent the landscape as a contemporary representation method, most readers will recognize that various media predates Adobe Photoshop and other computer-based graphic applications. Designers have consistently sought the latest technological advancements to aid the practical expression of their creative ideas."[18] Whether Humphry Repton's use of constructed watercolor perspectives providing his clients with "before" and "after" views in his famous *Red Books* or James Corner's blending of aerial photography, ink drawings, and collage materials to document the American landscape, the utilization of the latest available technology is a standing tradition within the design process or Dieter Kienast's composite garden drawings with textured collage materials to represent vegetation. The tools used to represent landscape influence and guide the process and creation of the built environment. What is noteworthy at this particular moment is the recognition that landscape is now being regarded as both a product and process, a noun and a verb.

Examples of mixed technique representation are the superimposition of drawings made by hand on top of others made digitally on separate layers, the use of a graphic tablet to have manual control of the tool, the simple juxtaposition of technical, pictorial, and literary languages, and, again, the modeling of materials such as sand on which contour lines can be projected through augmented reality. It is possible to use various techniques to enrich as much as possible the ways of conceiving, representing, and communicating landscape design - as Colafranceschi also points out - to overcome the dichotomy between the two modes of representation, to increase the interpretive skills of designers in using computer media, and to overcome the homogeneity of expressive languages of design. Thus, diverse languages are an opportunity for new physical and mental connections, and the most exciting processes are those of multiscalarisation and hybridisation. Detecting the importance of these aspects is an opportunity to realize how much more can be done. Exploring the potentialities of art languages applied to the project.

CHAPTER THREE

NOTES

[1] C. Lavoie, "Sketching the Landscape: Exploring a Sense of Place," *Landscape Journal* 24, no.1 (2005): 13-31.

[2] E. H. Gombrich, *Art and Illusion: A Study in the Psychology of Pictorial Representation* (Princeton: Princeton University Press, 1969), 17-35

[3] R. Arnheim, *Visual Thinking* (Berkeley: University of California Press, 1969), 10.

[4] Gombrich, *Art and Illusion*, 223-226.

[5] S. Vogt and S. Magnussen, "Expertise in Pictorial Perception: Eye-movement Patterns and Visual Memory in Artists and Laymen," *Perception* 36, no. 1 (2007): 91-100.

[6] R. L. Solso, "Brain Activities in a Skilled Versus a Novice Artist: An fMRI Study," *Leonardo* 34, no. 1 (2001): 31-34. The study shows, by means of magnetic resonance brain scans, which areas of the brain are activated in an expert and an amateur painter.

[7] H. Riley, "Drawing as Language: The Systematic-Functional Semiotic Argument," *Journal of Visual Art Practice* 18, no. 2 (2019): 132-144.

[8] *Ibidem*, 132-144.

[9] J. J. Gibson, *The Ecological Approach to Visual Perception.* (Boston: Houghton Mifflin Company, 1979).

[10] M. A. K. Halliday, "On Matter and Meaning: The Tow Realms of Human Experience," *Linguistics and the Human Sciences* 1, no. 1 (2005): 59-82.

[11] Á. B. Jónsdóttir, "Critical Thinking and Community Engagement Through Artist Actions," *International Journal of Art & Design Education* 38, no. 3 (2019): 700-709.

[12] B. Edwards, *Drawing on the Right Side of the Brain* (New York: Penguin Putnam, 1979).

[13] A. Brew, A. Kantrowitz and M. Fava, "Drawing Connections: New Directions in Drawing and Cognition Research," *Tracey* (2013): 1-18.

[14] M. Fava, "A Decline in Drawing Ability?" *International Journal of Art & Design Education* 39, no. 2 (2019): 319-332.

[15] M. Fava, "What is the Role of Observational Drawing in Contemporary Art & Design Curricula," *Graphicacy & Modelling* (2011): 129-141.

[16] Lavoie, "Sketching the landscape," 13-31.

[17] D. Colafranceschi, "Paesaggi di-segni, geo-grafie emozionali," *Ri-Vista* 19, no. 2 (2020): 68-79.

[18] P. Russell and M. Holland, "The Primacy of Hybridization within the Design Process: Thinking Through Making," in *Representing Landscapes: Hybrid*, ed. by N. Amoroso (London: Routledge, 2016): 103-104.

CHAPTER FOUR

The Creative Process and Design Education

The creative process is a physical and mental state in which artists or designers realize their ideas in an environment supporting them with the necessary tools, space, and time, along with the support of colleagues. It is a space in which it feels possible to create something without hindrance; in this sense, it is a state that must be consciously cultivated in the educational sphere. Doing so makes it possible to experiment with materials and have fun with them. In this "space" it is necessary for the worker to feel the urge to create, to experiment, and to do this he must be able to rely on numerous methods and techniques. The complementary and combined use of manual and digital tools is a way to give the designer a way to expand his creative and expressive abilities. Thus, the focusing on the relationship with the material aspect of representation can be an exciting creative experience.

Important work on combining manual and digital techniques – such as experimenting with mixed techniques to express conscious and innovative attention to the languages of representation in landscape design – took shape, particularly in the 1980s and 1990s. Every studio wanted to be on the cutting edge, express its originality, and communicate effectively to large population segments. Referring to this design period is crucial since the freedom and variety of expression available today derives partly from the innovations developed by landscape architects during those years, leading to considerable growth in the discipline. As Noël van Dooren writes, some important changes characterized this period. First, landscape architects began operating at the same level as architects and urban planners. Second, the landscape architecture profession reorganized itself into a dynamic world of offices and independent planners. Like architects, landscape architects have renewed themselves with a fresh and bright image, enabling their work to further contribute to an emancipatory leap in the discipline, partly thanks to new languages.[1]

After the success of the images of the Parc de la Villette, some studios began experimenting with visual languages; this trend was most evident in Holland between 1985 and 1995. Some focused on assignments related to urban open spaces and areas of new transformation, such as West 8, Lubbers, Quadrat, OKRA, and Karres + Brands. Others, such as H+N+S, Bosch Slabbers, and Vista, explored rural or large-scale assignments on infrastructure or water. Engagement in programs quite unusual for landscape architecture, such as wind power plants and peak water management, began.[2] During these years, designers also experienced the beginning of the transition from hand drawing to computer drawing. These factors led them to increase the use of different languages to represent designs, taking on increasingly larger dimensions. Adriaan Geuze, founder of West 8, and Bernard Tschumi were immediately confronted with the latest available technologies, with which they developed innovative images through pictorial languages close to deconstructivism. Bureau B+B's images, or Geuze's images of the Schouwburgplein, were considered as revolutionary as the work of Tschumi, who elaborated his Parisian project based on a deconstructivist scheme.[3] Through this research, software was developed, facilitating greater ease of use. However, different techniques were beginning to be utilized, combining various tools and allowing the emergence of hybrid landscape design styles.

Advances in computer graphics have begun to marginalize the role of manual drawing. With the desire to experiment, the relationship between material and craft interests and fascinates designers. In 1992, James Corner extolled the relationship of representation with materiality, writing, "Today's fascination with the visual image, the pictorial, precisely, makes it all the more important to recall how the greater part of landscape experience belongs to the sensorium of the tactile, the poetries of material and touch."[4] Peter Walker worked by drawing perspectives with an almost cartoonish technique in his 1997 project for Highbrook Park in Auckland. Jean Nouvel elaborated on drawings using photography as a basis for the 2001 Poblenou Central Park in Barcelona. Collages, especially, became very popular, as seen in the work of Archigram, among others, and later in the projects of the Office for Metropolitan Architecture (OMA) and Yves Brunier. Many considered collages a possibility for overcoming the hyperrealism of perspective drawings and renderings.

What better than the model, then, to experiment with different materials? As Niels De Couvreur reminds, any element can be used: plaster results in clean and artistic models, but there is also paper, plastic, foam, matches (Yves Brunier), and gummy candy (Martí Frank) - the variety of materials is almost endless.[5] To be remembered for authority is Kathryn Gustafson's abstract modeling. For her, the physical model enables adding essential material data to a project, something other visualization tools, she says, do not allow. This possibility proves crucial when working with landscapes, as the landscape architect writes in *Landforms*, emphasizing the use of clay, "The creation of landform demands the use of a connective material that responds similarly to the soil. That material is clay."[6]

The "material" taste must definitively begin to come to terms with what Jillian Walliss, in an article in JoLA in 2018, calls "digital tourn." It is beginning to take on considerable weight not only from an aesthetic point of view but, more importantly, because processing vast amounts of data is becoming unavoidable: "Big Data is understood as rapidly evolving data sets, often generated in real-time, and characterised by variety, velocity and volume [...] This unprecedented volume of information is shifting epistemologies in all disciplines."[7] There is growing interest in virtual reality (VR) and augmented reality (AR), ways of representing that interact dynamically and articulately with the audience.[8] Indeed, we need to consider that audience involvement plays a crucial role in the current design. This aspect is evident today, for example, in the method adopted by user experience design (or UX design), which draws on various aspects, such as visual design, programming, and psychology to keep users' needs at the center of design efforts. Artificial intelligence (AI) represents an other challenge that question again which are our aesthetic values.

Conversely, digital technologies can be an opportunity to overcome realism. The use of cartoon style demonstrates this. Cartoons use the three-dimensional model as an abstract, simplified basis for the essentials. In Agence Ter's example, it can be seen that all elements are abstract and very few realistic effects are used, characteristics that make it a style that is very much in vogue today. The cartoon style inspired, again, some striking images that appeared in the Poland Pavilion at the Venice Architecture Biennale 2021 Trouble in Paradise exhibition by GUBAHÁMORI + Filip + László Demeter. The group works extensively with this language to describe the processes of the contemporary landscape and the way they depend on successive events over time, the scale of which goes beyond individual perception. Their images are both evocative and communicative, referring also to temporality. That apply also to cartography. In the book *Terra Forma*, by Frédérique Aït-Touati, Alexandra Arènes, and Axelle Grégoire, this concept emerges clearly. It proves that we can gain a better understanding of some of the phenomena we are witnessing by improving our representational techniques. That also helps us understand some of the political implications of the Earth-system sciences and modern ecological thought by "mapping" some of their claims.

Landscape architecture has embarked on an exciting investigation process, renewing the link of design culture to the fine arts of previous centuries and producing many innovative images, some of which have even become iconic, such as those of OMA. Various techniques, such as augmented reality, video, cartoon, literature, and other forms of expression and combined representation, can be used as a rich and entertaining language. This capacity for language acquires considerable importance when we can support this diversity of expressions. However, to promote a rich and diverse landscape design culture, we must first consider the processes currently being promoted in education. The creative process must be cultivated from the level of education. In that case, it is crucial to understand what forms the creative process takes in teaching landscape architecture and how far new designers can acquire such tools to increase the quality of their design work and their opportunities for professional and personal fulfillment. To do this consistently and effectively, we need to set geographical boundaries. Analyzing the European context closely from a cultural point of view seems sufficient yet simultaneously vast and varied.

The academic context shows a considerable variety of approaches not only in design, as we have seen, but also in teaching, promoted by as many personalities as there are creators of exciting research. One of these approaches promotes the use and experimentation of digital tools. Recall, for example, Paul Cureton, professor of landscape architecture at Delft University of Technology and a partner in the OKRA studio. His interest in representation led him to work on integrating manual and digital techniques, such as geo-design and three-dimensional modeling. Like Cureton, designer Steffen Nijhuis, an academic and author of several publications on visualization, should be remembered for his research that privileges visual landscape and digital landscape architecture.

Christophe Girot, a professor of landscape architecture at ETH Zurich, is known for his research into the relationship between landscape architecture, topology, and new media in the analysis and perception of landscape. His work often places particular emphasis on very large-scale projects and land-modeling methods. We also remember him for founding a landscape visualization and modeling laboratory that has enabled significant advances in point clouds. Someone else from the same university who is worth mentioning is Günther Vogt, who, on the other hand, shows these diverse interests. Girot and Vogt adpot two distinct methods.[9] As we can see, the first achieves a high level of abstraction by relying on simulations from sophisticated tools, which can reproduce the tree's leaf as well as the riverbed. On the other hand, the second works preferentially with physical models, which it uses as a material experience to capture the behaviour and shapes of elements. In contrast to the first, we might call this criterion "material" because during the creative process, it becomes necessary to use material models, even in sketched form, to shape forms and bring ideas to life.

The third approach is what we might call "visual", in which perceptual and imaginative components are crucial. From this perspective, Simon Bell makes a significant theoretical contribution.[10] The visual and perceptual components are of great interest to him and serve as the focus of his publication *Landscape, Pattern, Process* and *Elements of Visual Design in the Landscape*. In this regard, we recall the work of Valerio Morabito, who has devoted many publications to the theme of representation, with the primary design process being based on hand drawing and imagination.[11] Some universities, such as the university in Versailles, are very committed to promoting the use of drawing in the creative processes of design. ECLAS frequently devotes a section of the Journal of Landscape Architecture to this issue, and it uses the annual international digital landscape architecture meeting held in Dessau to discuss innovations in digital technologies and their contribution to the discipline.

The educational scenario might seem sufficiently diverse and attentive to representation-related issues. However, we realize that, in the typical way of understanding teaching, this is only sometimes the case. To get a concise and reliable view, we can refer to the ECLAS guidelines for coordinating the content of different European disciplinary programs. The European Council of Landscape Architecture Schools has initiated two teaching-related projects: the Tuning Project and the EU-Land21. The Tuning Project defines the structure of European school curricula with general guidelines. It summarizes the method employed by educational programs for defining competencies and objectives to be achieved, and it clearly shows the learning and assessment methods adopted.[12] Relevant to this is the contribution of EU-Land21, which provides specific and updated guidelines for teaching development because of the continuous changes in the discipline in Europe and the demand for new programs.[13]

The criterion by which these programs are designed is in some way "constructivist," whereby the student layers information, concepts, and skills, then applies them in a real or, if academic, at least realistic context. A future landscape architect's academic and professional training consists of many aspects aligned with the many relevant skills in the curriculum. For the Tuning Project, these skills are divided into primary, generic, and specific.[14] The primary or basic skills comprise all the knowledge central to the discipline, such as landscape planning, design, and management. Generic skills are not directly related to the subject but are assimilated by students independently. These skills are then divided into instrumental (organization, analytical and synthesis skills, communication skills, problem-solving, etc.), interpersonal (critical and self-critical sense, ability to work in a team, ethical commitment, etc.), and systemic (putting theory into practice, research skills, leadership, initiative, etc.).

Meanwhile, specific skills are closely related to the subject and are divided into lines of learning, indicating the range of knowledge essential for the study of landscape architecture. For each competency (Basic, Theory, Process of Planning, Design & Management, Categories of Project, Vegetation & Materials, Tools, Practice), the EU-Land21 project flanks 12 learning lines related to them, which are then divided into technical details, content, objectives, outcomes, and skills to acquire.[15] In the skills-acquisition pathway, learners are expected to work alone or in groups, moving from possessing a few skills with a low degree of complexity to achieving increasingly elaborate skills. This is supplemented with hours of learning in workshops, excursions, presentations, seminars, and case study analysis. This cumulative learning system aims to lead the learner along a path of skill refinement so that they develop increasingly professional methods.

The first essential steps towards representation are outlined during practical exercises that are conducted in groups or individually. These exercises aim to train the student in sketching, traditional and digital drawing and designing, and using appropriate computer tools in the studio and workshops. Along the way, the student is taught to master specific modeling and design software and the techniques necessary to exploit them. Learning and reinforcing these skills constantly is an essential part of the holistic approach, which is so crucial to the discipline that it represents an actual generic competence. According to this perspective, in order to understand a subject fully, it should be considered in relation to everything that makes it up. The assessment methods also include the ability to concretize one's ideas into drawings and drafts as a compulsory skill to be learned and examined to determine student performance. In addition to completing written texts, oral exams, and reports, it is essential to prepare a project diary that contains an account of the work done, and it must be accompanied by detailed drawings. It is also necessary to produce a sketchbook of sketches and drafts made during fieldwork and used for the final evaluation.

From a holistic perspective, representation becomes an essential skill in the curriculum for enhancing visual communication, spatial thinking, traditional and digital drawing, software modeling, and so on. In this view, it is implicitly stated that aspects relating to perception and representation are fundamental. This confirms the need to understand the creative process as a channel of experimentation, integration, and inclusion so that students can elaborate ideas and values. It is a ground where they "stand" to understand phenomena and shape or reformulate them, as in Vogt's "material" vision referred to previously. From a methodological point of view, such an approach is beginning to establish itself by inspiring students' creative processes concerning landscape. However, it is not yet sufficiently addressed, so the "creative process" that is rarely mentioned takes shape. Thus, we find the inconsistency discussed in the previous chapter, highlighting the need to go deeper into the use of visual languages, which must be clarified for students to acquire. However, they are often mentioned.

In the ECLAS competencies, we see how little adequate space is devoted to representation, either as a creative process or visual education. If one excludes skills strictly related to landscape design (since they imply prior knowledge of the necessary techniques), there are few explicit references to representation. Indeed, the learning program considers this practice, but with other available methods, it has a marginal role. In sum, although representation is necessary, its specific role within landscape architecture courses is challenging to define. It still struggles to take shape as a creative process in the sense in which it was described. The mention of it always seems less than explicit, as if perception and visualization were a consequence of generic learning and other skills assumed during years of study. It confirms the validity, even in the teaching of landscape architecture, of the concerns raised by Michelle Fava's studies mentioned earlier.

Regardless of the guidelines analyzed, these trends can be generalized. The teaching of representation is often fragmented and discontinuous despite the need for more space devoted to creative processes and visual education. Several modules dedicated to drawing are needed, as more hours are needed to develop the required skills. The result – still a consequence of this practice – is that many students, if they still need to consolidate some visual education on their initiative by attending art schools or academies, do not learn to draw during their university studies. This fact carries considerable weight. The homogenization of landscape design languages that Weller discusses also depends on this. It means that extra effort is needed by students to achieve rich, varied, and quality visual expressions. However, such processes are increasingly being considered from a holistic perspective, at least from a methodological perspective, which bodes well. We also confirm that our direction is expressed in the first chapter. Perception permeates the field of landscape studies, and the study of visual education remains essential to developing critical skills based on conscious interaction with society and the environment. From view, we can imagine positive future developments: people feeling alive, creating by their hands something meaningful for their life.

NOTES

[1] van Dooren, “Drawing Time”, 145.

[2] Ibidem, 157.

[3] N. de Couvreur, *Evolving Visualisation: The designation of representational styles within the Acquisition of European Landscape Architecture,* Thesis, International Master in Landscape Architecture, Nürtingen-Geislingen University, 2019, p. 29.

[4] J. Corner, “Representation and Landscape,” *Word & Image* 8, no. 3 (1992): 243-275.

[5] de Couvreur, “Evolving Visualisation,” 29.

[6] K. Gustafson, *Landforms,* 2017, 7-18. https://issuu.com/gustafsonpor¬terbowman/docs/landform_-_gustafson_porter___bowma , consulted on 31 October 2021.

[7] J. Walliss, “Landscape Architecture and the Digital Turn: Towards a Productive Critique,” *Journal of Landscape Architecture* 13, no.3 (2018): 12-15.

[8] To understand the difference between virtual reality and augmented reality, the former is fully immersive and artificial, while the latter is an overlay of images and additional information to the reality in front of us.

F. Aït-Touati, A. Arènes, and A. Grégoire, *Terra Forma: A Book of Speculative Maps* (Cambridge: MIT Press, 2022).

[9] Both are professors at ETH Zurich.

[10] Simon Bell is currently a professor at the Estonian University of Life Sciences.

[11] Valerio Morabito is a researcher at the Mediterranea University of Reggio Calabria and Adjunct Professor at PennDesing University of Pennsylvania.

[12] ECLAS, *Guidance on Landscape Architecture Education: The Tuning Project* (LE:NOTRE, 2010).

[13] EULand-21, *Output 02: Guidelines on Revising and Developing Study Programmes in Landscape Architecture.* Internal publication (2017).

[14] ECLAS, *Guidance on Landscape Architecture Education*, 13-17.

[15] EULand-21, *Output 02: Guidelines on Revising and Developing Study Programmes in Landscape Architecture*, 13-14.

CHAPTER FIVE

Overcoming Homogeneity in Visualizations

Representation is a creative process in which invention is always possible. However, how can the homogenization of project languages be overcome? How can attention to representation be implemented in a vision aiming to understand the world's phenomena consciously and creatively? In this last chapter, after an articulated but necessary journey, an attempt will be made to answer our initial questions. First, let us recall that the need to represent the complex phenomena of an ever-changing planet has emerged; second, the need for greater awareness of the creative processes and languages of representation as a means of developing critical-interpretive thinking has become apparent. Both are centred on a more significant need, namely that of communication. Communicating today is one of the essential skills to focus on in design and teaching, and it can relate both to the effective transmission of the content of a work and the ability to establish various interpersonal relationships within work groups. On a large scale, communicating effectively means spreading a conscious culture of landscape design, focusing on relevant aspects, such as ecological values, and reaching broad population segments. The idea of the landscape gardener we saw in Chapter 2 comes in handy because it allows us to recover a curious and creative gaze towards nature aimed at understanding its values. Rooting, however, in the contemporary, we will highlight, in a synthetic way, some themes that represent opportunities or possible research projects in which representation can find enrichment.

In a 1977 interview, Gonçalo Ribeiro Telles said, "*O homem é o escultor do seu ambiente.*"[1] Today, the topic of representing ecological phenomena is more relevant than ever. This theme is fundamental since it means, in essence, representing the actual biological processes of a territory or a landscape rather than focusing on producing renderings and photomontages at the edge of reality. As Richard Weller writes in the article mentioned above on "hyper objects," if one looks at the images of many design competitions, it is clear that hyperrealism is the predominant mode of representation today. He argues that the increasingly immersive, high-resolution images are generally structured in a melancholy way, with a framed foreground, a central focus, and a background free of any urbanity or industry that would otherwise debase the bucolic ambience of the scene.[2]

Instead of indulging in what Weller effectively calls the "digital sublime," which is content to anaesthetize the audience, it would be far better to focus precisely on the processes of the Earth system. He concludes that to produce the landscape architecture of our time, we must face this challenge and attempt to draw realistic connections between the complex phenomena's macroscale and everyday life's microscale. One challenge for contemporary representation, as it also transpires from its discourses, is to engage the fourth dimension - namely that of time - and to show how temporal changes occur at various levels. It highlights how certain forms of human intervention will modulate, redirect, accelerate, or slow down changes.

Biological processes necessarily refer to the dimension of time, and this theme is relevant to this investigation. Noël van Dooren also recognises time as an essential aspect of landscape and its design in "Drawing Time. Concerning the representation of growth, change and dynamics in Dutch landscape architectural practice after 1985", he asserts that theory and practice are still less explicit about temporal aspects than they are about the purely spatial aspects of composition. For him, landscape architecture has not yet answered the question of how to represent time systematically.[3] For van Dooren, cyclical phenomena are a matter of primary interest. One thinks of water flows, as in Dreiseitl's designs, but also of vegetation growth, as in Michel Desvigne's design for Greenwich (2000). In the latter, the representations are effective and illustrative as they show, simultaneously in plan and section, the development of the trees that grow and thin out over the years according to the project's plan. As van Dooren writes, Desvigne's drawings show no final situation: "Desvigne's drawings portray the message that there is no final situation. There are stages, and these stages are equally important. It is interesting to compare this drawing with the earlier animated drawings."[4]

Therefore, the two-dimensional surface must represent both the third and the temporal dimension. In modern art, an example is Katsushika Hokusai's series of *Thirty-six Views of Mount Fuji*, made between 1830 and 1832; it is like Cezanne's Saint-Victoire or Claude Monet's four paintings of Rouen Cathedral from 1892 to 1894. The dynamism of a moving object can be represented as a superposition of the different positions occupied by the object in the same space. The best-known examples are Giacomo Balla's *Dinamismo di un cane al guinzaglio*, Umberto Boccioni's *La città che sale*, Eadweard Muybridge's chronophotographs, and Marcel Duchamp's *Nude Descending the Stairs.*[5] That technique could easily be used to describe flooding in a riverbed and the geographies it produces over time. In the last century, a technique for synthesizing different spatial and temporal dimensions was elaborated by Cubism, such as a collage of partial snapshots, portraying the object by shifting the point of observation in various directions in a mental recomposition. The collage is an incredible way to represent the landscape project.

At the same time, the issue concerning "patterns" must be considered.[6] As highlighted by some athors, by understanding the complexity of patterns as they occur in nature, we can have a greater awareness of natural phenomena and how to design them, from a small to a large scale. This issue is discussed, for example, by Simon Bell in the book *Landscape: Pattern, Perception and Process*. Bell states that nature's processes are robust and evident today. Landscape design should understand their complexity and multiscalar attributes, such as tsunamis, earthquakes, volcanic eruptions, heat waves, floods, and droughts. The discourse on identifying patterns as the recognizable structure of natural phenomena allows one to understand their operation in depth and, thus, design the landscape intelligently: "Landscapes develop and evolve through various climatic, geological, ecological and cultural processes. These processes shape the structure and character of the landscape which we experience. Over time, distinctive patterns emerge – ranging in scale from the distribution of small plants to the sculptured sides of a vast canyon. Our perception of these patterns goes beyond just their visual appreciation – beautiful though they may be – into a richer understanding of how we experience our environment."[7]

In representation, the concept of pattern is also frequently linked to modular grids. Plant leaves generally have axial symmetry, while flower corollas often have rotational symmetry. Axial symmetry provides the most immediate example. Folding a sheet of paper in half after pouring a drop of ink into it produces a spot of symmetrical shape with respect to the fold, which constitutes the axis of symmetry. Modular grids in geometry are a set of polygons that completely cover a plane without leaving gaps or creating overlaps. But modular grids can also include non-geometric figures, such as stylizations of leaves, as in Islamic ornamentation or the works of M.C. Escher or William Morris.

From geometric figures, one can move to organic ones, but in any case, modularity is a principle of economy that governs the development of nature.[8] This theme has interested architects such as Cesare Leonardi and Franca Stagi, who have developed a theory of land design they call *struttura reticolare a-centrata* based on the concepts of network, metamorphosis, and colour. In its practical application, the a-centered structure offers a possible writing of the territory where the dynamics of landscape formation and transformation are contemplated and interpreted through the combination of figures inserted at regular intervals. The a-centered structures are organized through a network system that seeks to respond to the crisis of rationalization of the territory by questioning the supremacy of the barycenter.

The transdisciplinary attention to the distinctive qualities of nature as a visual pursuit, in all its forms, gives us pause to think about the exciting advances made in scientific representations, such as botanical illustration: which today demonstrates remarkable aesthetic taste and impeccable scientific accuracy. We can think of Garry Fabian Miller, who repaints on photosensitive paper an exciting series of *Betula pendula* leaves, each with its own unique and recognizable pattern, or of artist Rob Kesseler, who manually reprocesses images of microscopic elements, such as the fruit of *Scabiosa crenata* (a small perennial suffruticose of the limestone walls of the

South-Mediterranean) just seven mm in diameter, which is photographed under a scanning electron microscope and then repainted by hand.[9] One also thinks of the recent docuseries *Tiny World*, curated by Paul Rudd, about the microscopic creatures that inhabit our planet, for its use of state-of-the-art photography applied to the knowledge and dissemination of natural elements. These same discourses are again present in Girot's representations at larger scales. For example, in the Ciliwung River Project in Jakarta, he analyses a major river through drone-operated three-dimensional reconstruction to predict numerous cyclical events related to river activity, such as water flows and floods. It demonstrates the importance of cyclical weather phenomena and allows new urban and landscape patterns to be simulated.

In the *Science* article cited in the first chapter, it was seen how satellite data today allows us to map soil transpiration, microbial biomass, enzyme activities, fungal and bacterial compositions, and chemicals released into the soil by decaying and living plants. Using the same method, for example, a recent project combined satellite tracking with fieldwork to map the habitat of the endangered Siberian white crane. Researchers found that these birds tend to avoid breeding where shrubs encroach on wetlands. Thus, with satellite imagery, the researchers could monitor the effects of flooding in dry summers to meet the cranes' needs. Landscape architecture, having outgrown interest in photorealism, can gradually handle more data, understanding and appropriately redesigning Earth system phenomena. In this process, it is possible to simultaneously include aesthetic and ecological factors, which underlie landscape design. It is also understood by Elizabeth Meyer in *Sustaining Beauty*, according to which beauty proves to be a vehicle for raising awareness concerning environmental phenomena.

These examples show the current interdisciplinary interest in celebrating the beauty of life in all its forms, also through representation.[10] Making the understanding of natural processes a visual research is probably what we need, using the artistic codes as a way of working with that knowledge in order to reshape our landscapes and environments creatively. The aesthetic component is relevant because of the values it can synthesize and convey, ecologically and humanly. Regarding the second type of needs encountered, there is a theme deemed worthy of mention: illustration as an opportunity for sensitive and personal expression. In this sense, it can be seen as a tool that successfully communicates concepts and emotions immediately, engaging in "dialoguing" with a broad audience.

Illustration is frequently considered a minor art, with secondary importance to the texts or works it refers to. In spite of this, illustrations play an important and unique role. Indeed, the most culturally interesting aspect of the project itself can occasionally be seen in the somewhat peripheral and more approachable expressions of designers' work. Moreover, this material is the most communicative part for the observer and the first to influence his thoughts and opinions. From this point of view, it is safe to assume that illustration is a tool that landscape design can equip itself with to establish a dialogue with users. Various "human" and "local" details that are occasionally missed are enhanced by illustration in the project. Therefore, representation can be understood as a tool for expressing unique ideas and "voices," emphasizing the peculiar and distinctive aspects of a landscape and carefully interacting with the environment. In reality, it's an antidote to the flattening in visualizations, as it fosters a closer interaction between places and users.

In a design conference held in 2019 at École national supérieure d'architecture de Paris La Villette, I argued that drawing has been the major technique of concept communication in a creative process that has produced many notable works of landscape architecture.[11] Reflection reveals a mindset that has set apart certain landscape architects.

This kind of thinking can be summed up as "designing by illustrating," which engages locals and people throughout the entire design process through illustration. For instance, Jacques Simon regularly employed this technique during the creative process. Simon was convinced that inspiration came from a perfect knowledge of places, made possible through a sensory relationship with the territory and its topography by creating many small and meaningful drawings.[12] This method was widely employed by Charles Moore as a project description and a foundation for design thinking. His output was full of vivid pictures of fantastical and dreamy settings, which eventually evolved into equally fantastical works. Watercolors, characteristic of the designer's language, allows him to dream, play, and make architecture without taking himself too seriously. Illustration, in this case, is an expressive component of the project. Similar approaches today are those of Michel Pena and Erik Dhont. Their drawings are capable of consistently linking representational practice to landscape design.

In the same conference, my opinion was that many designers held this opinion, even though it was not always stated explicitly and immediately. It was frequently done to overcome the homogeneity of the languages used to design. In a 2017 JoLA article, Australian landscape architect Anton James referenced this, stating that drawing entailed revisiting the location multiple times to fully capture its feelings because it crystallized the place's current value, gave it a voice, and allowed one to experience its future.[13] Illustration can even go so far as to be entirely conceptual, becoming an art form in its own right, as in the work of Danish Steen Høyer, landscape and garden art professor at the Royal Danish Academy of Fine Arts. In his *Global Gardens,* Høyer aims to provide an alternative to the interchangeable, devoured, preserved, or discarded pictures of current expressions. His creations embody authentic artistic endeavors that showcase the singularity of every perspective.[14] The concept is that from descriptive and realistic drawings to abstract and conceptual ones, illustrations often represent the most expressive part of the project. The designer can concretize his or her "material" and "sensory" activity, expressing authentic originality. Illustration can be understood as a tool that can stimulate the designers' inventiveness in the creative process. The mixture of artistic-pictorial and technical-scientific languages represents a remarkable enrichment.

The purpose of the representation of landscape design, as Angelo Dal Sasso and Darko Pandakovic point out, is the intellectual and emotional elaboration of space: "By representing a landscape, its contents, the organizational logic of a territory are extrinsic, the relationships and conditionings between orography and settlements, between vegetation and exposure, between crops and elevation are highlighted."[15] Additionally, drawing and cartographic representation are fundamental in landscape design when it is necessary to interpret reality and communicate these contents to stakeholders. It becomes increasingly necessary, therefore, to reflect on how to overcome the anaesthetizing superficiality of hyper-representations. Representing ecology means having a less superficial eye and returning to more meaningful images, just as having fun integrating illustrations as personal expressions in the margins of a project opens space for dialogue. In any case, there is still much to be researched. It is of particular interest, for example, to understand how to support different design stages through visual languages. If each requires a different execution criterion, developing strategies for effectively conducting the analysis phase, the master plan phase and the construction details phase may prove crucial.

Changes in scale over time, strategic design in teaching methods, and the fusion of manual and digital representations are other topics of definite interest for the immediate future. Mixed technique representation, in particular, as Nadia Amoroso reminds us, offers a break from the monotony in digital representation by which we are inundated and grants an opportunity to promote a unique style and character often associated with traditional sketches and handmade models.[16] In this connivance between different aspects that contaminate each other, however, representation is pushed to work more on integration and less on specialization, abandoning the idea of design as a definitive act and considering design action a continuous mutation. Further exploration of this research could facilitate an analysis of the available techniques and how each can help understand and manage environmental problems in public and natural spaces, that is, how effectively these theoretical orientations can be reflected in the design and which techniques prove most useful.

Nature represents an inexhaustible source of inspiration for representation - perhaps the main one. This representation becomes even more evident in understanding its workings and not just representing its forms, which are also unquestionably beautiful. Then, representation becomes a tool with enormous potential, almost as infinite as the possible combinations of techniques and approaches. In contemporary design, especially landscape design, this potential is little explored. Most methods adopted in architecture schools do not provide an artistic base and adequate education to train designers. A few brilliant examples certainly help us to be inspired, but still there is a certain flattening of languages, also due to an overly monotonous use of digital representations. Many tend toward hyperrealism and do not use representation as a personal interpretation technique. In short, designers can learn to "think" and "speak" more through visual languages.

Visual research, applied to design, combines scientific, cultural, technical, and artistic aspects to understand and manage natural phenomena. Artistic sensitivity is something extra, sometimes unnecessary, but can make a difference in contemporary design that aims to be increasingly communicative. The fact is that many things are understood through representation, which enriches us much more than we may think. This concept makes one understand why the current historical moment presents the designer with new problems and solutions, prompting them to seek forms of expression and question the role of representation. On the one hand, representation is a way to interact with an attitude aimed at understanding and observing to find a solution to a problem or answer a design question. On the other hand, representation's expressive character makes it a cultural expression, which sometimes flows into artistic expression, interacting with people's emotional, psychic, and sensitive spheres. Environmental challenges, the countless new theories emerging from various scientific and humanistic fields and social demands allow us to shed new light on representation and pause to understand its irreplaceable role, mainly when applied to understanding natural phenomena and nature's transformation. Visual languages can help us establish new and virtuous relationships with the landscapes around us. Thus, we must start by devoting more time and resources to education's creative processes. These are essential values for a landscape design culture that is alive and full of desire to research, understand, and innovate.

Representation is experiencing an unprecedented phase. The most exciting aspect is that, in feeling the aim to effectively transform the environment, we enjoy the creative process with the knowledge that any recourse to different styles can be valuable, and that it is always possible to innovate. The process resorted to seem, in some ways, "kaleidoscopic" Somewhat as in the Baroque style, which inherited new conceptions of space from geometry, astronomy, and mathematics, today's representation seems to want to grasp the new that is advancing from every branch of knowledge to arouse an incredible desire to discover, to transform and to amaze. Drawing, however, remains something fundamental. As Nadia Amoroso writes, "While not photographically real, the drawings express a sense of flexibility, offering openness to the designed landscape and leaving the viewer with a sense of imagination and wonder."[17] Even outside official channels, drawing is a source of great passion for young landscape artists and - we continue to emphasise - fun. Worthy as an example is the work of Linescapes, a group of talented recent graduates who move inventively in Berlin whose work is oriented, through the use of various platforms, to inspire and instruct students in different techniques of manual representation applied to the landscape. Starting with the provocative expression "Why your Art sucks," step by step, they guide trainees to develop their creative potential to the fullest.[18]

Education research also comes with many promising possibilities. As Colin Gray and Martin Siegel suggest, reasoning about drawing is a form of reflection-on-action.[19] This concept answers the questions raised in the introduction about representation's role in our profession and society. In this view, the process is more important than the outcome. The obsession with competition and results can give way to reflection and recognition of values to be promoted, making life in design studios more sustainable. With their imperfections, human drawings become an expression of spontaneity and establish a greater connection with users, denoting original styles. Indeed, achieving technical perfection today is easy, but an authentic expression based on an intelligent and empathetic attitude is more appreciable. Institutions can create a secure space so communication becomes more conscious, intimate, and spontaneous. Representation can become, for all intents and purposes, a form of mindfulness, that is, a practice of the "here and now" that consciously seeks what it most needs (or likes) to meet the needs of life on this world, whether aesthetic, ecological, or cultural.

NOTES

[1] G. Ribeiro Telles, *Textos escolhidos* (Lisbon: Argumentum, 2016), 25.

[2] Weller, "The Hype of Representation," 30-39.

[3] van Dooren, "Drawing Time," 130.

[4] *Ibidem*, 166-170.

[5] P. Odifreddi, *Abbasso Euclide!* (Milan: Mondadori, 2013), 18-20.

[6] Patterns, in this context, are understood as structures recognizable by a certain regularity and repetition in the landscape and natural phenomena.

[7] S. Bell, *Landscape: Pattern, Perception, Process* (New York: Routledge, 1999), I.

[8] V. Valeri, *Nuovo corso di disegno* (Venice: La Nuova Italia Ed., 2005), 64-65.

[9] R. Kesseler, *Plant: Exploring the Botanical World* (New York: Phaidon, 2016).

[10] E. Meyer, "Sustaining Beauty: The Performance of Appearance, A Manifesto in Three Parts," Journal of Landscape Architecture (italicized) 3, no. 1 (2008): 6-23.

[11] R. De Marco, M. Poulot and O. Jeudy, "Introduction General," in *Dessin, Design, Projet: Représenter er Reconfigurer les Espaces Ouverts,* École national supérieure d'architecture de Paris La Villette, ed. by R. De Marco and M. Poulot (Florence: Firenze University Press, 2023), 34-35.

[12] E. Falqui, "Ricordando Jacques Simon," *Ri-Vista* 14, no. 1 (2016): 130-141.

[13] A. James, "RE: DRAWING," Journal of Landscape Architecture 12, no. 1 (2017): 44-59.

[14] S. Høyer, "Global Gardens," Journal of Landscape Architecture 1, no.1 (2006): 59.

[15] A. Dal Sasso, D. Pandakovic, *Saper vedere il paesaggio* (Novara: De Agnostini, 2009), 218.

[16] Amoroso, *Representing Landscapes,* 3.

[17] Ibidem, 1.

[18] Linescapes, https://linescapes.de, consulted on 4 January 2022.

[19] C. M. Gray and A. M. Siegel, "Sketching Design Thinking: Representations of Design in Education and Practice," *Design and Technology Education: An International Journal* 19, no.1 (2014): 48-61.

CONCLUSION

To reflect on the relevance of the creative process in the field of landscapae design education, we started aknowledging that the concept of landscape is linked to processes involving perception in its complexity, in the close relationship that man establishes with nature. There is also visual reworking, which is not considered reductive compared to ecological and social factors, for example. Cultural interest in landscape originated also in painting, and we cannot resort to the term defining it and not think about the fact that the act of painting a landscape and recognizing it have been dependent on each other. Not surprisingly, from Pope and McHarg to Weller, "redrawing" nature, albeit with different visions, is a recurring motif. This tendency leads the discipline of landscape architecture to take an interest, with a renewed passion, in shaping the environment around us to deal with planetary changes and crises. Representation is crucial in interpreting the world and its complex transformations. Thus, the need to refer to the digital world emerges since, in this complex context, it allows us to consider a significant amount of data. This, however, is both an opportunity and a challenge. Using such media often turns more to image production than to reasoning and only sometimes helps to utilize all the possibilities software offers.

Following the reflections of researchers such as Riley, Jónsdóttir, Lavoi, and Fava, we saw that representation involves a complex mental and emotional process, fulfilling the functions of a language. Therefore, it must be considered a vehicle for understanding the phenomena of the world through which landscape values are defined. From this perspective representation can be considered the space for interpreting the world. Therefore, drawing and sketching become crucial expressions of project communication, through which critical and personal reasoning can be formulated. Representation is a means of awareness. Despite this, the current inclination in teaching is to take this aspect for granted. The educational system could be focused more on creative processes at all levels. This is particularly evident even in education guidelines, where it is difficult to identify the specific role of representation within landscape architecture courses. Perception and representation are a consequence of generic learning and other skills assumed while studying. This practice means that many students cannot learn to draw during their college years if they have yet to consolidate some visual education. Meanwhile, most students show considerable interest in visualization techniques, the languages of which they often learn as self-taught students.

Showing potential, meanwhile, is an interest, at least from a methodological perspective, in an attitude that considers the whole range of activities performed by the student. Indeed, from this viewpoint, perception permeates the field of landscape studies and the study of visual education remains a crucial aspect of developing critical skills based on dynamic interaction with society and the environment. Visualization also has introspective value for young people, who tend to consider it a tool for understanding their inner selves and affirming their identity. Moreover, learning appropriate methods and tools is essential to finding satisfactory employment. Therefore, representation could be given more significant consideration in the educational system.

Considering recent theories studying perception-related cognitive processes, design can take a big step forward by continuing research on inspiring and guiding appropriate creative processes. These could consider the "human" and "material" aspects of representation to bring more quality and depth to the design. Therefore, it seems essential to use visual education to combine various manual and digital techniques, encouraging as original an expression as possible. This would also be useful in applying to the new design challenges. To emphasize these aspects - attention to terrestrial phenomena on the one hand, to communicative and interpersonal ones on the other - and to overcome the homogenization of languages, we can focus on the representation of natural systems and illustration as an expressive complement to design. These themes are the fields in which sensitivity, awareness, and creativity meet, creating an optimal living and personal vehicle for effectively communicating human needs and those of Earth's system processes.

To continue, as noted above, other themes to research are changes in scale, changes over time and the hybridization of manual and digital. This shows that we are in an unprecedented phase, not only of design but also of its representation, in which drawing remains a fundamental practice. In this context, representation can be seen as a form of awareness based on languages and processes that allow us to become conscious interpreters of our time. The number of existing manuals on the subject is increasing every day, just as frequently as advances in technological innovations in the discipline are published. What we intended to do instead, as made explicit from the beginning, is to offer an alternative view on the needs to be considered in research and teaching activities. Reflection on the role of representation in landscape design not just allows us to shed light on creative processes to make them more stimulating, effective, and in touch with current needs. It also becomes an opportunity to explore our new relationships with nature, questioning how we describe and conceive them.

This aspect opens numerous opportunities for this discipline. Artistic languages, when applied to design, are crucial to being interpreters and observers of the world's phenomena. Landscape architecture today is more aware of its role in a complex and ever-changing planet. Designers dedicated to these challenges have a great opportunity — a world to explore, understand, describe, design, protect, and transform. In this active quest, representation can contribute to its historical background and many technological innovations. As researchers we could devote more time and resources to the creative processes of education to recover activities and values essential to stimulate designers' creativity, as much as it happens in art and music schools. Students need guidelines that support them in using existing representational techniques, reminding them how much can be done, researched, and innovated. Also teaching could emphasize the development of such creative skills in young designers even more.

Finally, to answer the initial question of why representation makes us unique observers and interpreters of reality, and why it adds quality to the creative process of design today, we can assume that representation it is possibly an indispensable creative process in today's world. It represents an opportunity to develop critical interpretive thinking, a form of awareness that allows us to create deep reciprocity with the landscapes around us, with their cultural, social, and ecological aspects, and to interpret these values consciously. In order to represent and communicate the landscape project effectively, it seems appropriate to enrich this process by resorting to all kinds of experimentation to promote - somewhat as in the gardner artist's multifaceted enjoyment - a varied culture that integrates multiple languages, from the small to the large scale and from the personal to the societal sphere.

Nurturing the creative processes as a physical space, as an experience in which we spend time together engaging in artistic experiences, could be a possible solution in for turning alive our education system. With that approach it is possible to renew in contemporary times the peculiar attitude of the landscape gardner, from the scale of the garden to that of the Earth. The curiosity to know and the desire to shape nature constitute an approach rooted in aesthetics but which proves, at the same time, a real opportunity to shape the world around us. Beyond the technical use of the tools at hand, what is most needed is to understand what gaze to adopt, what role to take, and what attitude to emphasize because that can enrich our research. That experience amplifies these possibilities when we decide our point of view and the method by which we pursue our goals. Landscape design can consider the representation as a valuable opportunity for inspiration in order to conceive meaningful relationships with natural elements that can be investigated, known, and designed in connection with nature. As Merleau-Ponty says in *L'Œil et l'Esprit*, "What is called inspiration should be taken literally: there is really inhalation and exhalation of Being, respiration of Being."

AFTERWARD
BY VALERIO MORABITO

I have closely followed Daniele's work during his PhD research on representing ideas and design in landscape architecture. This book is a natural outgrowth of his research: synthesizing and elaborating ideas and information that find their coherence and clear and timely legibility. He entered the world of landscape architecture because he wanted to understand the meanings and forms of the image, representation, and design of gardens, parks, and public spaces: this has characterized and continues to characterize his work continuously and consistently.

It is clear that this book has chosen a difficult field of research because the representation of our ideas has spanned eras, cultures, and the arts, eluding any static definition. The moment it found its own form or meaning, representation had to instantly relate to new techniques, new cultural needs, different social conditions, and new expressive syntaxes.

Umberto Eco, in his *History of Beauty*, masterfully explains how beauty and its representation (inseparable concepts) have traversed human history in the evolution of its arts. In order to paraphrase Eco, the landscape is beautiful as an aesthetic and cultural idea, and its representation is the representation of its beauty. Like beauty in art, it has ever-changing boundaries that are impossible to define precisely. From a painting to a photo, from a literary composition to a sculpture, from architecture to a garden or park, representation is a creative constant of human knowledge and imagination.

However, the representation of a painting is the synthesis of its components: technique, form and subject. The same thing happens in poetic composition or the writing of a book. In contrast, when representing landscape architecture, there is a process of design stages, from the representation of ideas to the technical representation of the project to the representation of its realization. In the latter case, as John Dixon Hunt often teaches us, it is materialized by the photographs or descriptions made of it by its visitors and users.

The text addresses the issue of the representation of landscape architecture by explicitly addressing a topic of great topicality and debate, both in the world of the academies and the world of the profession. He does so by explicitly stating his desire to investigate the representation of ideas in a longer process, leading to the definition of a design for a garden, park, or public space. However, it does not merely explain, with specific and numerous examples, the evolution of the representation of landscape architecture over time. It aims to inform us that this stage is fundamental to the creative process and contributes significantly to developing imagination for creative design that can stand out in an increasingly homogenized cultural landscape. Among the many arts, landscape architecture has significantly benefited from the evolution of digital technologies that, with the advent of Artificial Intelligence, are becoming dominant in landscape design's creative and imaginative process.

Instead, Daniele explains well how drawing ideas in a cultural context like ours becomes an avant-garde tool - perhaps the primary avant-garde tool for new creativity and imagination. The book does not take refuge in nostalgic reminiscences of drawings made by landscape architects with artistic skills. However, it suggests that the drawing process can evolve into a hybrid, dynamic, and multidisciplinary process. In this context, the pen, pencil, and brush are tools with autonomous forms of expression that often add meanings other than the authors' intentions.

They contain exactitudes and inaccuracies, precisions and errors. If digital tools have the accuracy of data as their first and last goal, the drawing tool admits error, and error is always a gateway to evolution.This book embraces the imperfection of freehand drawing and its errors, affirming and supporting their fundamental role of disruption in the evolution of the contemporary creative process. Expressing thoughts and ideas independently and collaboratively with the siege of digital tools.

BIBLIOGRAPHY

MAIN REFERENCES TO THE DISCIPLINE

N. Amoroso, *Digital Landscape Architecture Now* (London: Thames & Hudson, 2012).

S. Ballard, *Art and Nature in the Anthtopocene: Planetary Aesthetics*. (London: Routledge, 2021)

S. Bell, *Landscape: Pattern, Perception, Process* (New York: Routledge, 1999).

A. Brew, A. Kantrowitz and M. Fava, "Drawing Connections: New Directions in Drawing and Cognition Research," *Tracey* (2013): 1-18.

T. Calvano, *Viaggio nel pittoresco: Il giardino inglese fra arte e natura* (Rome: Donzelli Editore, 1996)

D. Colafranceschi, "Paesaggi di-segni, geo-grafie emozionali," *Ri-Vista* 19, no. 2 (2020): 68-79.

J. Corner, "Representation and landscape", *Word & Image*, 8, no. 3 (1992): 243-275.

P. D'Angelo, *Filosofia del paesaggio* (Macerata: Quodlibet, 2010)

A. Dal Sasso, D. Pandakovic, *Saper vedere il paesaggio* (Novara: De Agnostini, 2009)

E. Falqui, "Ricordando Jacques Simon," *Ri-Vista* 14, no. 1 (2016): 130-141.

M. Fava, "What is the Role of Observational Drawing in Contemporary Art & Design Curricula," *Graphicacy & Modelling* (2011): 129-141.

M. Fava, "A Decline in Drawing Ability?" *International Journal of Art & Design Education* 39, no. 2 (2019): 319-332.

C. Girot, "The Elegance of Topology", *Landscript* 3 (2013): 79-116.

S. Heyde S. "The French Picturesque and the Invention of Landscape Architecture as a Design Discipline," *Journal of Landscape Architecture* 12, no. 3 (2017): 76-87.

S. Høyer, "Global Gardens," Journal of Landscape Architecture 1, no.1 (2006): 59.

J. D. Hunt, *The Figure in the Landscape: Poetry, Painting and Gardening during Eighteenth Century* (Baltimore: John Hopkins University Press, 1989).

M. Jakob, *Il paesaggio* (Bologna: Il Mulino, 2009), 30-55.

A. James, "RE: DRAWING," Journal of Landscape Architecture 12, no. 1 (2017): 44-59.

Á. B. Jónsdóttir, "Critical Thinking and Community Engagement Through Artist Actions," *International Journal of Art & Design Education* 38, no. 3 (2019): 700-709.

C. Lavoie, "Sketching the Landscape: Exploring a Sense of Place," *Landscape Journal* 24, no.1 (2005): 13-31.

E. Meyer, "Sustaining Beauty: The Performance of Appearance, A Manifesto in Three Parts," Journal of Landscape Architecture (italicized) 3, no. 1 (2008): 6-23.

A. Metta, *Paesaggi d'autore: il Novecento in 120 progetti* (Firenze: Alinea, 2008), 138-139.

F. Panzini, *Progettare la natura. Architettura del paesaggio e dei giardini dalle origini all'epoca contemporanea.* (Bologna: Zanichelli, 2005), 45.

H. Riley, "Drawing as Language: The Systematic-Functional Semiotic Argument," *Journal of Visual Art Practice* 18, no. 2 (2019): 132-144.

M. Russo, "Multiscalarità: dimensioni e spazi della contemporaneità", *Archivio di Studi Urbani e Regionali*, XLVI, no. 113 (2015): 5-22.

R. Salerno, *Paesaggi Forme Immagini* (Milano: Libreria Clup, 2006), 9.

N. van Dooren, "Drawing Time: The Representation of Growth, Change and Dynamics in Dutch Landscape Architectural Practice after 1985," PhD diss. (Academy of Architecture Amsterdam, 2017), 161-162.

J. Walliss, "Landscape Architecture and the Digital Turn: Towards a Productive Critique," *Journal of Landscape Architecture* 13, no.3 (2018): 12-15.

R. Weller, J. Ho, "Planet Photoshop", in *Landscape Architecture*, 4 (2015): 4.

R. Weller, "The Hype of Representation: Some Thoughts on the Roles of the Hyperreal and the Hyperobject in Contemporary Landscape Architecture," *Ri-Vista. Research for landscape architecture* 19, no. 2 (2020): 30-39.

F. Zagari, *Sul paesaggio: Lettera aperta* (Melfi: Libria 2013), 104-112.

Fig. 1. Fraser Halliday, *Plaszow visualisation*, credit Nadia Amoroso, 2016. The image evokes the Romantic attitude toward nature, seen as a mystery to be contemplated, as in Caspar Friedrich's work *Der Wanderer über dem Nebelmeer* (1818). The hybridization of manual and digital techniques represent a good opportunity for innovation in visualization.

Fig. 2-3. Ana Horhat and Silviu Aldea s renderings. Visualization can be a way of combining different styles of representation and referencing the languages of the fine arts. In that case, the use of subjects from art history as references makes the visualization of the contemporary project particularly interesting. Also the colors are kneaded and spread without using pure colors, and with a tincture similar to the one used in the preparation of the canvas in traditional oil painting.

Fig. 4. Fabio Di Carlo, Alfonso Giancotti, Monica Sgandurra, Andrea Grimaldi, with the collaboration of Daniele Stefàno and Samaneh Nyckayin, Giardino di Ercole Vincitore, *Piranesi Prix de Rome*, 2018. The images fuse images from the past and the future, reasoning on the symbolic value of the landscape and its potential. The contrast between ancient and contemporary languages can be an interesting way to overcome the homogenization of visual languages.

Fig. 5. Atelier Crilo, *Etna,* illustration, https://www.ateliercrilo.com/architectural-visualization-rendering. The image is a mixture of manual and digital techniques, a method that seems to revive the classical charcoal sketch and color drafting. This use of digital tools demonstrates the potential for great expressiveness when traditional techniques of freehand sketch are embraced. The act of drawing can always be a site-specific action, also painting *en plain air*.

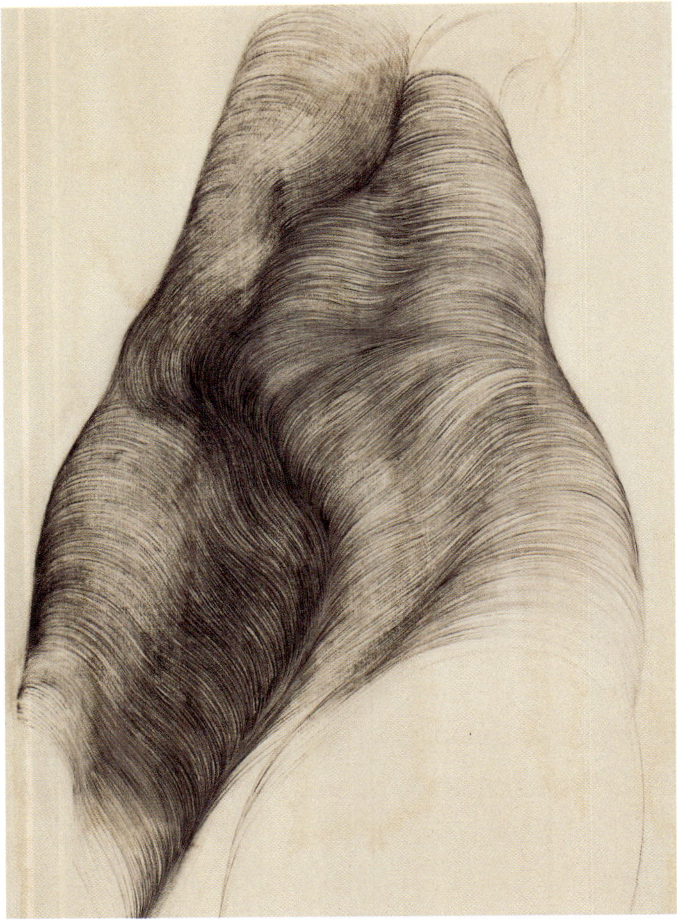

Fig. 6. Christine Enrègle, *Jardim Botânico da Ajuda*, charcoal on cotton canvas, 2021. © Christine Enrègle / ADAGP. Christine Enrègle's drawings show how drawing is a tool for investigating environmental phenomena and not just for reproducing a static reality. The stroke, which recalls a Leonardo technique, captures the vital and dynamic aspects of plants, understood as evolving bodies.

Fig. 7. Valerio Morabito, *Memory of Landscape*, from the exhibition "Composite Land-scapes", Isabella Stewart Garden Museum, Boston curated by Charles Waldheim and Andrea Hansen, 2013. Morabito's productions are an example of how hand drawing can describe identities recognizable in the landscape. The images depict inner memories that are projected on the natural forms, shaping people's perception of the place, a story made by association of impressions that comes to consciousness. At the same time the imagination is a way to establish new relationship with the place.

Fig. 8. Matthias Oberfrank, *Landschaftsfenster Sülztal zum Schloss Eulenbroich, Rösrath*, 2021, City of Rösrath.
Fig. 9. Gero Engeser, tong+, *Der neue Stöckach in Stuttgart*. (Frankfurt a.M./ Hanoi) with Hannes Hörr Landschaftsarchitektur (Remseck), 2019. First prize.
The images are an example of how to overcome hyperrealism in renderings and how to "talk" with users and transmitting emotions. All works are visible at www.landstrich.eu.

Fig. 10. Christine Guérard, *Teufelsmoor 1*, 2017, Kakemono.
Fig. 11. Christine Guérard, *Lava, Sometimes quiets the moss*, 2016.
The temporality of natural phenomena can stimulate our research on available representation techniques. The pictures try to understand and describe peculiar aspects of a place and its temporal dimension through the use of pictorial languages.

Fig. 12. Daniele Stefàno, *Con l'Arte e con i Fiori*, 2010, mixed technique. Special mention, *Premio "La città che vorrei"*, 2010, General Commissariat of the Italian Government for the Shanghai World Expo 2010, project on the theme "Better City, Better Life". The project argues that Art and Craft ideal is not an something relegated to William Morrison's time and that the pursuit of beauty is a practice that is confirmed out of time and style as a human necessity.

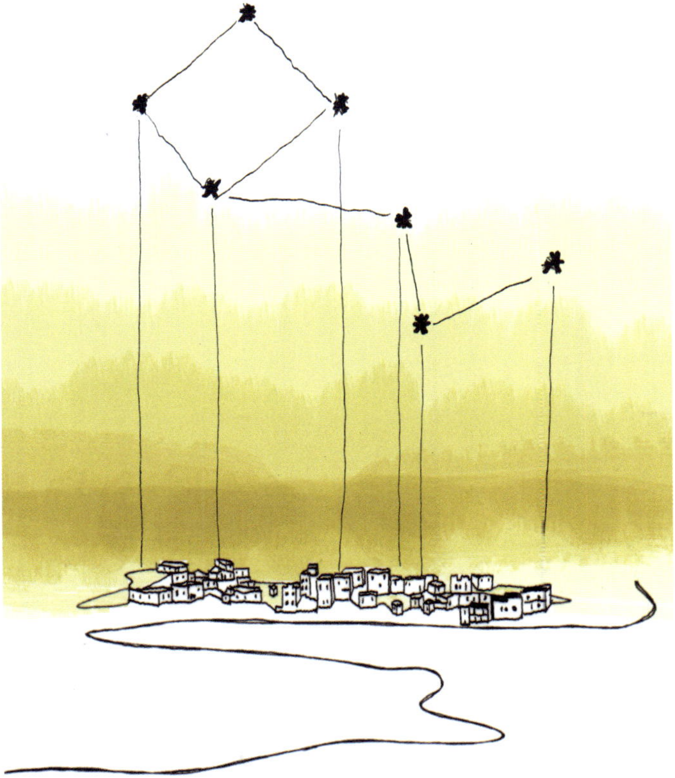

Fig. 13. Daniele Stefàno, *Andria*, series of illustrations from Italo Calvino's *Le città invisibili*, mixed technique. Published in Fabio Di Carlo, *Paesaggi di Calvino*, Melfi 2013. Drawing illustrations of Calvino's cities was an opportunity to discover how much potential this kind of work can have when transported into landscape design. The illustrations proved to be an opportunity to go beyond the superficial view of reality, investigating, researching, and bringing to light something that is perceived but not always visible.

ACKNOWLEDGEMENTS

This book is the result of a PhD thesis in Landscape and Environment, Sapienza University of Rome, concluded in 2022. It was realized thanks to the contribution of several people. First, I want to thank my tutors, Isotta Cortesi, Elisabetta Cristallini, Alfonso Giancotti and especially Fabio Di Carlo, without whom I couldn't have learnt a lot about the discipline of landscape architecture in the last few years. I want to thank Valerio Morabito for his willingness to exchange constructive and stimulating ideas, Ellen Fetzer for the the Doctoral Colloquium ECLAS 2021 and Nadia Amoroso for the concession of pictures from her books. My sincere thanks also go to Simone Antonelli for the cover image, Christine Enrègle, Christine Guérard, Ana Horhat, Matthias Oberfrank for the concession of their artworks, to Maria Letizia Zozi, Ludovica Marinaro, Caterina Dragone and Daniele Politi for their support.